Oxford F

David Constantine is an authority on Hölderlin, as well as a poet and translator. His *Collected Poems* was published by Bloodaxe in 2004.

Bernard O'Donoghue teaches medieval English at Wadham College, Oxford, and has published five books of poems, of which the most recent is *Outliving* (Chatto 2003).

Also available from Carcanet/Oxford*Poets*

Oxford Poets 2007

an anthology edited by

David Constantine and
Bernard O'Donoghue

Oxford*Poets*

ℂARCANET

First published in Great Britain in 2007 by
Carcanet Press Limited
Alliance House
Cross Street
Manchester M2 7AQ

A CIP catalogue record for this book is available from the British Library
ISBN 978 1 903039 70 0

The publisher acknowledges financial assistance from Arts Council England

Typeset by XL Publishing Services, Tiverton
Printed and bound in England by SRP Ltd, Exeter

Contents

Introduction

This is our fifth OxfordPoets anthology. On the back of the first in 2000, we said we had 'no editorial programme or ideology beyond a desire to represent the best', what we found 'most compelling in terms of formal and rhythmic invention'. That was all we said; the volume contained nothing but poems and the names of the poets: no manifesto, and no biographies except – ironically – the information that the wonderful poet who concluded the anthology, Rebecca Elson, was already dead. The intervening volumes have been slightly, but only slightly, less reticent. Our introductions were still very brief, and to the same effect as the blurb quoted at the start here; we gave short biographies of the poets in the fourth anthology to provide a context for the poets.

There has been a longer gap since that fourth volume than there was between the earlier ones, so this is a correspondingly bigger anthology with seventeen poets in it, far more than before. Our approach here is editorially more expansive as well, though this does not represent any change in our principles and priorities. The poets have written their own individual introductions. Some have chosen to offer a kind of *ars poetica*, saying what they write and why; others have introduced the poems one by one, leaving them to reflect their composers' views and motivations. We think the resulting range is very thought-provoking, but that it also conforms to our original priorities. What our poets here have in common is commitment and a seriousness of purpose, whichever part of the poetic world they operate in. It is an old idea in poetics: a faithfulness to the truth of experience in the very diverse kinds of writing represented.

Many of these writers touch on the twentieth-century concern with the intersection of the public and the personal. Serious writers can't be indifferent to the plight of the outside world. Hilary Menos is a nature poet with concern for environmental damage, even if she declares a wish not to be thought a 'tub-thumper'. Sue Leigh's poems place the anguish of personal bereavement in the wider imaginative experience of the bereaved and anxious women of her family in the course of two world wars. Adam Hansen's visits to Macedonia caused him to resume writing. He links this to his Serbian grandfather, but also to the literary world which he studies and teaches. Still, he concludes that 'conflict is not universal, or inevitable, but induced or inhibited by historically specific factors'.

Other ways of regarding history and the political world are represented here: Catriona Clutterbuck, descended from Cromwellian settlers, lives in South Tipperary with her English husband and English–Irish daughter, travelling out to teach English in an Irish university. No wonder she feels and resists 'the tug of nostalgia', or dwells on the importance of place – one of the great subjects of modern poetry, not least in Ireland. Frances Thompson writes, often with acerbic wit, out of the same loyalties to places, shared between Devon and her native 'strictly divided community that was 1960s Ulster'.

There are different forms of miscegenation too, of a less politically explicit kind. John White also comes from Ulster and acknowledges the importance of the provincial, seen as an 'oral culture sadly drifting away'. His powerful sense of the local is displaced on to various cosmopolitanisms: to sociological concern for children with disabilities, and to distant worlds. Like many of these poets, he is not sure why he writes, but takes his inspiration wherever he finds it, 'knowingly or otherwise'. Anna Robinson, likewise, takes her inspiration in response to a more immediately social community, living and dead. Olivia McCannon lives in Paris and translates between French and English. She finds that operating in French has taught her 'the uses of economy, and the dispassionate distance needed' to write in one's own language. Again, she is typical in her widely defined sense of what 'community' means in our century.

Diverse as all these writers are, this description is already unduly procrustean. Many of our poets don't fit any of these categories, loose as they are. Maybe 'form and rhythmic invention' is, after all, all that unites them. Kieron Winn has an eloquent commitment to place, but his Lake District is as much a literary as a geographical location. Something similar is true of Damian Walford Davies, whose Wales is founded as much in pictures as in place; Miriam Obrey's sense of 'place, myth and local history' is her common inspiration, but her explanation of the individual poems takes in Mandelstam and Klimt – a variation on ekphrasis, to borrow Walford Davies's explanation. Lynne Wycherley's poems are irradiated by light, but it is the painterly light cast by particular places, such as the Orkneys.

And of course other poets – ultimately perhaps all the poets –

see their poems primarily in relation to the particularities and privacies of their own experience. Some of the most intriguing self-profiles seem to consider the occasion of the poems for the first time: Jemma Borg's exploration of the place of science and incantation (which sounds so different) in her poems; Hugh Dunkerley's reaching for a Housman-like prickle as the starting point of his elegiac poems. Saradha Soobrayen sees her poems as conceived in the dark, the unquestioning nature of which she finds comforting. All the same, this world of a 'language not fully arrived at' provides a frame for the compressed discussion of five hundred years of colonial history. Jo Roach lulls us into a false sense of readerly security by saying she does 'a lot of cleaning and tidying up' by way of preparation, before talking about the consolatory power of poetry after the stillbirth of her first baby.

Maybe that is the indispensable strength that is particular to poetry: its capacity to come partially to the rescue when events are at their most demanding. The last poet I want to mention has the same place as Rebecca Elson had in the first anthology, seven years ago. The celebrated novelist Grace Ingoldby died too young of cancer last year. We are honoured to have a group of her poems here and very grateful to her sister Mary for introducing them to us. On Arvon courses Grace was an inspirational fiction tutor, but she always had an eye on what the poets were doing too. Her poems here show why. We are proud to introduce these poets; they all show – Grace most poignantly – how poetry can help by striving to be, in Seamus Heaney's great phrase, 'adequate to our predicament'.

David Constantine
Bernard O'Donoghue
Oxford 2007

JEMMA BORG

Jemma Borg took a first in zoology at Oxford and has a D.Phil in genetics. She has worked as an English teacher overseas, an environmental researcher and a science editor. Her poems have been published in a number of magazines and are included in the Poetry School anthology *I am twenty people!* (Enitharmon 2007). 'The mathematician' was first published in *Mslexia*; 'Soul sends a letter at last' in *I am twenty people!*; 'Do I still think of you?' in the *Asia Literary Review*; and 'How it is with the circle' in *Oxford Magazine*.

'Science means simply the aggregate of all the recipes that are always successful,' wrote Paul Valéry. 'The rest is literature.' There is at least the rhythm of that thought in my poem 'The mathematician'. I wanted to write something of how it feels to do science (science really wants to be maths, it seems to me), working under that historical assumption that there is an independent reality 'out there' to discover. But while science may look into the world with senses we do not have, the mind still seeks to understand what it is already enmeshed in – and what is 'out there', what is 'other', is sought like a beloved.

Much of what I write is dialogue, direct or implied. This might be anything from the long tradition of 'soul' talking with 'body' to self talking to itself, as perhaps in a mirror, or with other poets and with their addressees (in 'Do I still think of you?', the dialogue is with Hopkins's god as addressed in 'God's grandeur'). This is why I sometimes write poems in two parts – as in the two sonnet-pairs here. It's a sort of dialectic process – one part taking one view, the other another, trying to move from contradiction to synthesis or, perhaps, action. I'm thinking of Rilke's 'stretch your practised powers till they reach between two contradictions', and also of Mikhail Bakhtin's 'we never speak in a vacuum'.

Perhaps in reaction to experimental science – or augmented by it – I'm interested in techniques that encourage 'random', non-logically-obtained first drafts (although the linguistic philosopher George Lakoff would say that, because of metaphor, a poem is still a rational being). Though I don't tend to use other people's work or found texts, the poem 'Do I still think of you?' does mix my words with those of Hopkins. In other poems, such as 'A century of ravens in flight', I've tried to use collage to get behind the surface of language and to generate a rich texture which can then be used to serve the lyric impulse. Whether one decides to argue for a 'use' for poetry or not, I still think of it as spell, as incantation. To return to Rilke, poetry must 'make a temple deep inside our hearing'. He does not say in our 'ear' but in our 'hearing' which is a mindful, thinking, emotive, body-centred activity, rather than something more passive.

The mathematician

From his window, he could see snow falling as the fractals
he couldn't see but which he relied on being there.

How could he predict numbers lost at the far end of his imagination
like countries so far away he'd never make it to them?

He sensed a shadow falling, heard a soft thump of snow
and, then, a crack of glass. Below, against the conservatory,

an icicle as pure as an organ pipe, fat as a stalactite made of diamond,
had shattered into its pieces of supercooled clarity.

He thought of her skin: it was as translucent and seductive
of light as ice. It was impossible to talk to her.

On a sheet of paper, he wrote the first of a series of equations:
numbers teaming up as water does, irresistible to itself

in the cold, numbers running through snow like the parallel tracks
of a sledge, and soon his page was filled with their writhings,

their shorthands, constructs and passwords. On the other side
of the horizon, houses began switching on their lights against the dusk

and he also reached for his lamp. There were some things
of which he could be certain; the rest was love.

Soul sends a letter at last

Ah, you should see the light in Alexandria,
above the harbour, in the hour before noon.
I arrived here on Wednesday by train from Cairo,
the seats very generous in first class.

For a while, I was unsure of who I was
– the heat can be disconcerting – but I was glad
to be carrying a blanket, the air conditioning
rather chill after the desert, and even a dirty sea

would have been welcome, although that was
not what I found. Everything in the Sahara
had been one colour: the camels, the giant bricks
of the pyramids. It's only the sky that orientates you.

The ascent into the belly of the great Cheops,
to the small space they called 'tomb'
but where no king's swaddled body
was ever found, was as disconcerting:

was I travelling to the stars or burrowing
into the earth? I know your ear has been listening
for this letter, for its solemn little rectangle.
I'm sorry it's felt very silent, but so it is

we become mothers to each observed detail
of our separation and it's only at night
we miss one another, my dear. In the day,
I must confess, I barely remember your name.

Do I still think of you?

after Gerard Manley Hopkins

I

I do still think of you but the feeling is lean.
   The world cannot gather its grandeur
or share things with us, and we cannot feel
   our bare being nor the rod of nature
on our bent backs. We do not rate spring;
   nor have we ever been so bleary-eyed.
We say: it is last, it is out, it is over. Sometimes
   we are sure our explanations are enough

to scratch the questions, but we are spent
   on the brink of emotion. Generations of sentences
brood and toil their difficult trade, your ghost
   holy and foolish, walking its silent thoughts
through the walls and into the nights.
   Now the world's feet, and ours, are shod.

II

My feet still think they are ears to the ground,
   shod with shining foil-wings for walking
with the bright-fantastic to the charged
   soil in the east. It's as though they can hear light
gathering fine and careful next to me. The world
   is seared in freshness; pearls of night ooze like oil
before the dawn, everything that was brown, pruned
   as in a sketch, becoming almost and then actually

becoming, like love bent and shaking warm
   from all the stuck corners, creating a day
which wears its grandeur without a man's
   crushed voice. This is not bare work, but a rod
of will and a plan, and it is the sun now setting
   out and out, collecting itself, westward.

A century of ravens in flight

'Why is our century worse than any other?'
                                    Anna Akhmatova

You were right: it was a century of ravens
in flight, a thousand crosses revealing
nothing of the graves chalking the mud
in the intricacies of daylight, nothing

of the grief dividing the breathless black
of night or the stench of hair behind
the mirror's image. The road took possession
of the woods like autumn and we drove

its zig-zag in a shining ulcer of a car.
At first, we could still see the trees
above our passage but then they became
only the spaces where light was unable

to pass and then it was just the clouds
that lurched at the lowering sun. To ourselves,
we were neither secret nor forbidden,
our eye in the rearview mirror

partitioned from our face. Where could we go
for relief? Our fingers plunged into the fabric
of our seat. You were right: it was a century
of ravens in flight and still we drove

as though there was a spare world of air
in the corners of our mind we could reach
on the westward route, though this was a lie
even the dark would not be able to hide.

How it is with the circle

I

Actually it's just a line, but all points
are equidistant from the centre,
without distortion, and that's what makes it
special. Contained by and within that line
are all the attributes of circularity:
the infinite exactitude of π,
a circumscribed, two-dimensional disc
too correct to be a moon or an eye,
but sure enough to be a wheel. It's a special
kind of curve, then. Not the curve of a skull
or a country's anxious border. It's starker
than that, less porous, unbreached and a pair
of compasses can swing a black lead
circle on a page pretty double-quick.

II

But we haven't come nearly far enough.
What does a circle become if you puncture
it? All curves and arcs, sections
of construction, lines and roads and scars.
Did Euclid even consider this? Tiny
arcs rejoining to make circlets
which wander off like untethered balloons,
hopeful as helium, for a moment
like soap bubbles carrying their own rainbows.
And the insides seeping out, all that
was circle, into the circumambient
messiness of air, the unpredictability
of blood and time. How it is that flesh wants
to be something else – how it wants to be more.

CATRIONA CLUTTERBUCK

Catriona Clutterbuck was born in 1964. Her poems were published regularly in the early 1990s; she began to write again in the past few years. She won the 2005 Start Poetry Chapbook competition, published as *Ghosts in My Heels*, and a place in the Oxfam (Ireland) 'Poems for 2006' Calendar competition. 'The Dry Mouth' won the 1995 Oxford Poetry competition, judged by Seamus Heaney, and is planned as the title poem of her first collection. 'By First Firelights' and 'The Pond Field' were first published in *Windows, Altars and Artists: Introductions* (Series 1, Windows Publications 1994). 'The Dry Mouth' was first published in *Oxford Poetry* 8 (2).

My home is in rural south County Tipperary in Ireland, where I've lived for most of my life. I'm married to an Englishman and we have a small, independent daughter. I grew up on a mixed farm, a middle child among six in a family descended from Cromwellian settlers, who made their home in a townland between two distinctive villages – hilly Ballingarry, sitting on top of a flooded anthracite fortune and location of the desperate cabbage-patch rebellion by the Young Irelanders in the famine year of European revolution, 1848; and low-lying Mullinahone, home of Charles J. Kickham, Fenian revolutionary and author of *Knocknagow*. This book was revered in most Irish homes up to the mid-twentieth century for its proclamation of the credit of the little village against the forces of legalised unjust depopulation. Life happens in the cracks between identity plates – or so I say on my commute to my job in a Dublin university, where I teach Irish writing and then catch the train home. I see that the four poems chosen for this anthology are preoccupied with what can be retained of the security of home when this has already disappeared. I see my parents head-and-tailing these pieces, holding out for good faith with all its costs. I taste the tug of nostalgia, too sweet yet craved in my bones. I see that my childhood is remembered for me here, more than me remembering it: a film played on the collapsible screen of poems, at the ground level of a world. My work is drawn to the intersections in time and place of the lives of those closest to us – to how often strange is that which is most familiar in them; how already familiar, that which we meet as strange. The recurrence of kindness, especially when it is least justified, is a thing that interests me. I think it may be linked to our right to make-believe, and can be found in what some poems do.

By First Firelights

1

Where the grain of the table runs, the surface peels.
The bench fits close to the yellow wall;
early evening sits comfortable in the window.

I am fitting into this day like early days,
stepping big-step into the yard, step into the garden,
child. Return down the furrow of years

slow spinning yourself to sleep. Your mother
is working near, nursery firelight on the red wall
where her shadow bends to your peace each minute.

This is the second hand that scales the air of thirty years,
old ashes in the cracks of the fireplace back, grained in.
We do not, then, carry this world on our backs –

oh the world, this day, is carrying me.

2

I was a wet eel in the stone kitchen sink,
the white clawed bathtub too far and too big.
I slipped inside my mother's hands
to be lifted two steps to the towel
that aired on the chair by the fire,
and shadows grew from the bulb in the ceiling.

An eel was in the rain barrel by the shed
they told me – 'monster, keep away, don't look in';
one day my brother held my legs and I peeped,
saw sluggy green, bluey brown, eyes of red:
saw it move like oil at my scream.

3

Conspirators by the red ash of the kitchen,
my grandfather at seventy and me at three;

it's dead of night and we are quiet listening
on one waxy ear-plug each to the BBC.

Above our heads, rush of footsteps, urgent orders –
doctors and my mother's scream of pain:

small shadow slipping silent down the stairs
through cold hall and door to her big chair

to stretch bare feet to the heat with an old man,
touch skulls to the voice of the world's service.

4

You would lay the length of your self
on the high broad mantle over the fire,

playing hide-and-go-seek in its light,
so each child could slip their own shape.

In the cold window the starry yard
and the fir trees feathering the moon

watched them hunt you through the dark hour
you lay silent over crackling wood,

unfound, and getting lonelier not to win.

The Dry Mouth

There was my brother and me
bringing eight heifers home
from Modeshil for the mart
the day before I left for England.

We came to cloudy black sloes
in the green branches above us.
'Can you eat those?', I asked.
'Do you remember nothing at all,' he said,
'from when you were a child?'

So I bit in and got the dry mouth
that I'd forgotten for years.
I sucked at it over The Islands bridge,
the road bright in the sun, the leaves still on.

I put three berries in my pocket.
I knew this morning would come,
lying in a new bed after dawn,
sloes nuggeting in my mind
against the dry mouth.

The Pond Field

The cock pheasant shot skyways from Brigid's Cross reeds
in the pond field we stalked as children, palming flies
with long grasses from the still brown lid of the water,
inletted. Each journey there, squelch and suck of
black wellington stuck and tug at it with both hands, panicking
and there was a day I stepped out into muck and went skittering
around the velvet wet, the sodden earth, in my skin
or if there wasn't such a day there could have been;
it must have been spring mostly – jamjars, on the hunt for spawn
– so my jumper's always too hot, the wool slightly steaming
or the field steaming, in the first real heat of the year
baking crusts on the clay cliffs at the water
where cattle's feet had scored deep the dank edge.

These measurable acres around the house are staked
and latticed to the heart – that place and those times,
the brownheaded child that slides like a film across my brain,
myself or part of me, more like myself than me,
coming back after years in stamped prints from my skull,
slipping free and floating right-side up to my side.
Insects dance on the meniscus of the past. 'Pastoral,' you will say,
'the choreographed sun-squints of memory.' 'Palming flies,' I

will say,

'from the still, brown surface.'

My Father Making Shapes for his Grown Children, Visiting

Cue his stage-entrance crash through the warped back door,
the wall behind him dinted with care,
into the kitchen where we laze over late tea and toast –
'Make a shape! There's the world to do out there!'

His work litany reloads that's taught us all to run
daily exercising anxiety
round the dog-track that we've carved about the edges of the
                                                    undone,
coming home only ever provisionally,

making shapes out of the city, driving from Dublin,
easing the clutch of our commitments into stories
of his hope in us as gone beyond him, stranded and stumbling
in the dark passes of his Athy or Castlecomer.

– Seven-months' child, you crossed too early your own line of fate,
hating your full-term never-self's shiny achieving,
but also sensed how you'd pass by that other making shapes,
your ideal life and your real one intermingling

on the ground we stand, holding your shadows to our throats
in light sideglancing across time's messy table
towards a child's hand drafting fate in a thread from your
                                                    work-coat,
the shape of our lives from your tangled cat's cradle

whose slipknot solves as sudden as the morning's cool and grey,
as the cement paths we tread spill slowly over
into the spring-cusped yard of home on this translucent day
where you make for the warped back door –

HUGH DUNKERLEY

Hugh Dunkerley has published two pamphlet collections, *Walking to the Fire Tower* (Redbeck Press 1997) and *Fast* (Pighog Press 2007), which includes 'The Transit of Venus' and 'Vernon Street'. He has been a Gregory Award winner and a Hawthornden Fellow, is currently West Sussex Poet Laureate and teaches at the University of Chichester.

Author photograph reproduced by permission of James Simpson.

For me a poem usually begins as something almost physical, a feeling of excitement which coalesces into a few words or lines. At this stage I will have only a vague sense of what the poem might be about. The writing process is then a matter of trying to uncover what it is the poem wants to say. All kinds of things can get in the way of this: ideas about what a poem should be, my conscious opinions. But when a poem is successful there is a sense of having gone beyond what I know. Sometimes it can take months or even years to finally finish a poem. When I am asked what I write about, I find it hard to give an answer, as I don't have any agenda or theme of which I'm conscious. However, looking back at my recent work, I can see that there is a strong elegiac strain, an attempt to look at what death and loss actually mean. I am also interested in the ways in which we are both a part of nature and radically separated from it. Poets have long been fascinated by nature, but what we understand by nature today is very different to the Romantic understanding of it. Finally, I believe poetry is still relevant and important because it retains the ability to replicate the complex nature of experience without giving in to the kinds of explanations that ideology and mass consumerism push on us every day. It is a space in which we can contemplate the ultimately mysterious nature of existence.

Vernon Street

In your sister's dream your father
is skating on Vernon Street,

alive again, the darkened road
one long tree-lined rink.

He is alone, carving perfect turns
in the unmarked ice, the hiss

of his skates the only sound.
The houses pass: the one on the corner

where his mother lived;
your sister's old flat; number 11

where the young widow would
run her hands through his teenage hair.

He knows the dead are in there,
waiting for him,

but for now he still has time
to make use of the old skates,

the leather straps creaking
with each thrust, the thin blades

singing on the ice,
the whole frozen street his own.

The Guardians of the Water

for Chris

They came in the middle of the night
– three old men he'd seen at the bar
and thought nothing of –
banging on the big wooden door,
asking for the señora,
not even meeting his eye.

His wife, wrapped in her dressing gown,
still tidying her hair with one hand,
spoke rapidly in Spanish,
and led them down to the kitchen.

Standing by the sink, he felt excluded,
just as he'd done at that bullfight,
the crowd seething round him,
his head aching from the heat,
the trembling bull, bloodied and exhausted,
collapsing in the dirt.

Then one of the old men produced a sledgehammer
– from where he couldn't imagine –
and with a soft thud
knocked a hole in the back wall.

In the semi-darkness he could hardly make them out,
the three of them
crouched by the white-edged hole,
muttering something about drought,
the old Arab water course that used to run below the house.

They said little as they left,
just grunted to his wife
and were gone.
He wanted to know who was going to pay for the plaster,
but his wife shrugged, said she was sleepy
and that she was going back to bed.

The next day, walking in the garden,
he was sure he could hear the sound of running water,
detect its clear metallic tang –
like the smell of an English summer day after rain –
among the hot scents of rosemary and thyme.

Early Warning

Suddenly the bees deserted the air,
the hives fell silent
and the garden filled with an absence.

Meanwhile the numb flowers
went on offering up their sweet surfeit
to nothing and to no one

and he scoured the skies
for some dark unseen threat.
Later, as he was planting the first

of the new potatoes,
the rain came, running in rivulets
down his back, soaking his shoes,

drumming on the hives like hail.
That evening, on the news, he heard
about the stricken reactor,

thought of the potatoes in their darkness
ticking with danger,
of his own wet skin, how by morning

the bees would be swarming
at the hive entrances,
yearning for nectar.

Bantam

He greets me,
a raucous grating issuing
from his brilliant throat,

the whole feather and bone
frame convulsing
as if trying to choke up

that domineering shout.
The eyes go wide,
the yellowing bony beak gapes,

and it happens again,
this lung-straining yell
splitting the mid-morning calm,

mastering him.
Utterly its instrument,
his small tatty wingbeats

clap the air
in ineffectual protest.
Subside.

He settles the glossy ruff
of his neck,
shaking his tiny reptilian head

as if waking from a trance,
begins to pick jerkily
at the ordinary corn I've scattered.

The Transit of Venus

In the blue dusk yours is the first light,
acetylene in the southern sky,
eclipsing everything except the moon.

I used to see you as the earth's cool cousin,
your orbit holding hands with ours
as we swung around the sun,
just beyond the reach of its fiery breath.

Now our telescopes watch
as you crawl across the sun's face,
little more than a cinder.
Below clouds of sulphuric acid,
your five hundred degree surface
is blasted by magma, cooking under a greenhouse
of runaway carbon dioxide.

I think of Jupiter, crackling with radiation,
the stone-cold corpse of Pluto,
the thin veil of our atmosphere,
its lie of blue.

ADAM HANSEN

Adam Hansen grew up in the Yorkshire village of Blackshaw Head, and has taught at universities in England (York and Oxford), Poland and Macedonia. He is currently Lecturer in Renaissance Literature at Queen's University Belfast. He has published poems in *Oxford Magazine, Aesthetica, Cadenza, South, The Frogmore Papers,* and *Other Poetry.*

Before I wrote the poems collected here, I hadn't written any for years. My experiences in Macedonia meant I started again.

Perhaps it was Skopje. If you can fall in love with a place like a person, then I fell in love with that city. In sound of its mosques, in sight of the Millennium Cross on Mount Vodno, passing building plots and war memorials, on streets quilted in summer's dust or winter's drifts, or coming back home at dawn from clubs to my flat in Kisela Voda, I was often faced with the city's sensations, yet also by déjà vu. With the intensity of the present, my mind tried to tell itself it had seen all this before. This was only half-untrue. Growing up with a Serbian grandfather who'd fled Tito, I was sensitised to, if not totally sensible of, the complexities of 'Yugoslavian' cultures. Macedonia was uncanny – foreign yet deeply familiar, not least in language. Picking up fragments, I heard strange echoes I didn't know I'd forgotten. And teaching literature at Tetovo's innovative multi-ethnic university, I'd translate English commonplaces into terms the students understood, learning the strangeness of my own tongue. Perhaps the literature I taught had an effect too. By design, poetry connects. As the students found new ways to talk about and beyond the conflicts of their communities, old English prosody found odd forms.

Perhaps also it was because I realised how people and places are made by powers great and small. Catching a breath after Yugoslavia's disintegration, Macedonia's diverse communities sustained a fragile peace, and the future was – is? – unclear. Yet despite darkness, there was abundant warmth and light and life. People got by, surviving as they do. Conflict is not universal, or inevitable, but induced or inhibited by historically specific factors. That said, conflict is not discrete in space or time; but neither is compassion. So though the poems' titles locate them, I hope the poems themselves suggest why we might look again and deeper at relationships between people, times and spaces too often forgotten.

Weathering

Lake Ohrid, 10 April 2004

She weathers, smiles, wet-eyed, skin of wax, and
talks of her pension, her grandson at college;
glances from the entrance to the chapel
beneath the cliffs in spring's still early dark,

from the faint fading candles and saints
and towels she's laid, now damp on the floor
under cracked panes the lake lashes through,
to wintered over boats up by the shore.

She endures, making peace with the water
among rocks more water than rock, rushes
and red-rooted willows

Skopje, 17–18 March 2004

After Mitrovice, during Iraq

North of here, war goes on.
A scab is picked and bleeds
someone adds injury to insult
and all hell breaks loose.
Tit for tat turns ugly
then '10 to 20' dead.

We deploy idioms to savage precision
calm inoffensive at 6 or 9 o'clock
and keep the troubles local;
confess our civil tongues cannot describe
surrender to the untranslatable
and desolate history's collateral.

Decorous distinctions are defended;
borders and distances mapped, determined.
Their aberrance is naturalised
our normality upheld.
East of here, war goes on
with words and arms and men we cultivate.

Skopje-Tetovo, 11 November 2003–Summer 2004

Poppies blow brilliant where earth is disturbed,
marking ploughed fields, fresh graves, sickled verges,
but spreading like split lips spill blood that scabs
and trickles; heavy-headed yet sleepless,

nodding, by moaning roads, at Polish tanks.
They dessicate as summer turns to dust
shaking seeds in a scratchy death rattle
(the pencil in John MacCrae's dispatch book).

Most soldiers and the nurse remembered here
survived the shells and malarial heat,
made Skopje, late summer 1918,
but died from flu after Armistice Day.

From Ypres to Skopje and Tetovë
there are no fields foreign to afion, lulëkuqe,
poppy.

*Note: 'afion' and 'lulëkuqe' are respectively the Macedonian and Albanian words
for poppy.*

Lake Ohrid, 28 July 2004

I wait in line, pay 10 denars, and look
through a telescope catching sight of the moon.

Dazzled, I see
nothing but white; and then my eye changes;
and then intense white and night beginning,
seas, scars and striations, the shadows cast;

each passing car and kid make the moon shake
and shiver fragile, flutter, ripple, live,
textured and moving, a moth's wing in flight,
mirroring deep silver shades of the lake.

Skopje, 20 June 2004

From across the river
dawn's call to prayer is lost
in birdsong and water.

From up on the hill
the lights of the cross flicker faint
and with sunrise, fade.

In noon's heat, the crosses and the minarets
cast some of many shadows
clear and dark.

Kisela Voda, Skopje, Summer 2004

They go out walking late each night,
him, tall, straight but inclined to
her, limbs contorted, itching,
raging with the day.

After the shop shutters rattle fast
the water trucks pass by,
spraying the gutters and pavements
to keep the dust of summer down.

They're still walking in this mist,
as day's heat fades.

GRACE INGOLDBY
1949–2005

Grace Ingoldby was born in Winchester in 1949. She lived in
Northern Ireland during the 1970s and wrote for the magazine
Fortnight and the *Belfast Telegraph*. She wrote five novels and a
study of the Island of Sark. Her freelance work included teaching
courses at Arvon, Winchester Art School, Winchester Prison and
Broadmoor. She won prizes for her novels, short stories and her
poetry. She had three children, Lucy, Tom and Patrick.

Grace thought that her poetry was the best of her work. It was vital to her. She worked and re-worked, through different genres and the scanning and rhythm words. Her reading was wide and eclectic, she looked at everything with a writer's eye, never without a notebook and a pencil.

One of the things I miss most about her is her original response and interpretation. Discuss an idea with Grace and you always came away with something entirely new. She was clever, extremely amusing, and quick to cut through the pretentious and the worthy.

She'd laugh about it, but I was always very impressed with what she was interested in at any given time. She'd say, 'I've got this absolutely terrible book which I totally adore.' *The Complete Monk*, for example – I mean, who else would read it, and is there even another copy?

I want to be true to her and to remember what she loved and what she found inspiring – any opportunity for the sea and swimming, birds definitely, flowers, Italy, the Romans, looking in skips, the hedgerows, the weather, London and life.

Fortunately, I recorded her reading shortly before she died, and I pushed her to explain a little of the inspiration behind her work. So I paraphrase below what Grace said about some of the poems included in this anthology.

'Book of Settlements' was inspired by reading the Icelandic Sagas. Grace described them as being 'written with the flat of the hand', masters of understatement where accounts of mass slaughter would be followed by 'many things happen in the late evening'.

'Restrictions at Delphi' is a lament informed by the laments of Ancient Greece and Sicily. Grace was caught by the pragmatic reportage of life lived.

'Blackbirds from the point of no return' came from images of Pompeii, the wonderful diver in the graveyard at Taormina in Sicily, and reading about Alexandria.

'As still as this' has Hockney's deep blue pools, and the recollection of being literally stopped in your tracks by an image or a view which takes you straight back to another place.

Most importantly, to me, to her, to all her family and friends, is that here is some of the work, printed at last.

Mary Ingoldby

Suddener than we fancy it

Snow starts as love does, uncertain whether
to go on. Talk of it softly, say it
melts like white sugar on the tongue. Espousing
detachment see it speckle the ditches
marking the margins it may later obliterate
specks of it slipping between mother and
daughter, between bramble and alder; fluttering into the
arms of the scrub oaks, beneath which the wind
flower waits. Watch as the snow spots the grey
herons who, flying from different directions
pair here every year. Fly into the thoughts of
mother and daughter, disturb them with images
that rock in the water. Somehow they must settle
and settling steal themselves, not to watch the snow growing

Afternoon harries the hopes of the
morning, snow lies on the hangings, snow in
the open takes down the pegs between
the earth and sky. Vain to remember, in
the silence that's mounting, how only this
morning, the sounds from the beach reached here; they
heard sea water roll over stones. At five
before five the gods make a pragmatic
departure, the temperature drops, it snows
harder. Snow razors the ridges, is this
what 'too late' is? All encompassing sprawl
and no wits about you, when night mimics
day and you can't find a way to go on.

As still as this

Dive into Mediterranean pools
mix with Mediterranean fish, float
above tesserae laid for you, reckon
how right you were about these pools, how they

summed it up. Drift: lying as still as this
allowing the past to slide through fast, then
coming abruptly upon yew trees, black
as this water's blue. In the deeps love

rises, though the heart's been rinsed a
million times since, though hope has been
decanted. Now light withdraws, as if you'd
spent it and softly the evening comes, floating

its owl songs, this evening is full of it
'Hoo-oo-hoooooo'; the tawny owl, 'Boobooboo'
the short-eared owl. Dark slugs of yew where there
are only cypresses. How the heart slips
towards them, knowing it can feed there for a while.

Blackbirds from the point of no return

Boy made in mosaic, you could easily
ask him, or ask the bronze diver who stands
on his hands, stand on both of their shoulders
to peer through the sky, for it looks as though
the weather's closed in.

Believe it, we won't now see any bird
this evening and the questions we prepared –
with our elbows apparently – now run
down our arms and out through our hands
into the waters that fill the four harbours.

For now we must walk the shaded, arcaded
streets, acknowledging friends who are here at
this time with us, divert them, encourage
comfort, confess how you almost forgot
the appointment to meet where they mend the

umbrellas and get their shoes heeled at the
shop of the stocking man with his display
of gleaming inverted limbs, silkened up
to the thigh in deniers to die for. How, why
and wherefore, our place in the scheme

of bird things? Are you Alexandrian?
Are you or were you, once part of a part
of us, something for us or from us, you
the most precious of all prepositions
for with us, undoubtedly, you are.

Wren of wrens

Big birds went first so he had this. Behold
A tiny shred of life on which to hang
When the heat tormented, when nights were cold
He would recall the notes the small bird sang
From saltbush, tree top, gully scrub: all day
And even when the sun sank in the west
He chirruped while the others flew away
Determined to continue without rest
Inside his tiny body flamed a fire
It filled his throat and shone from his bright eye
Persisting though he was by nature shy
To sing unaccompanied by a lyre
His message for all lesser specks was strong
Forget the other warblers, sing your song.

Morning be salve to you

On a clear night let the stars be your alibi
Save yourself from yourself by throwing your
Head back, gazing at something many light
Years away, for whatever happens in
This position it is impossible
To cry. Cryers bend forwards, they hug and
They hide themselves, tears leave them ragged, their
Sadness seeps inwards to what's already
Sodden. At dawn the cocks crow from the grey
Of the orchard you're leaving; morning be
Salve to you, day be square with you, fair with
You, remember to throw your head back should
Sadness still have its hands on you, for in
This position only the cockerels can cry.

Book of Settlements

And so time passed with fine settled weather
On the bleach green the women stretched out the
linen, pulling it taut till it slapped in
the freezing air. No news to report failed
absolutely to staunch what she told him.
The aggravations of a day watching
linen, geese coming on like an army
pulling and tugging the grass. Along the
indented coast she asked for him, with an
eye to the tides she checked through the driftage
the sea carried east. The fear never left
her of losing what she alone could see
in the folds of the linen, when shadows
fell on the linen, the shape and the size of his hands.

Christ in the Wilderness – Consider the Lilies

Beetles hunting other beetles pause
This is a named field changed
Softly indented, two equidistant
Dips, two rounded craters, should they skirt them
Or explore?

A word or two up on the rim, about
Keeping together, about young blood
Crawling in, then out, of crater two, one
Has an inkling that something of this
Afternoon should be recorded. How the
Dandelions and the daisies there, the
Meadow vetches in the grasses were seen
To be unbroken, simply bent and the
Atmosphere, the heaven scent

Heat lingered in the indentations made
By two great knees, two outspread hands.
A rabbit sprawled in the warmth collected
That evening, daisies, dandelions vetch
Their petals stretched wide open, and in
The English twilight hares came leaping
Naming the craters for a new game played
There, crying the name in the air and leaving
It there

Night and moths reconnoitre, bats scoop and
As the last bee flies towards the bank, comes
Darkness and no glimpse of any moon. What
Happened in that field today? No method
To record or prove it. God came and the
Flowers stayed open late.

Restrictions at Delphi

*'Nor was it permitted to lay down the bier and wail at turnings in the road
or outside the houses of others'*

By name then, the man calling the cows and
how the wood looked in April, consider
the celandines and coltsfoot at that time
of the year. Specify it was the voice
of Stebbings calling, call that carried with
a practised kick, over the buckle where
the hedge bowed out with a thorn tree and an

alder. Water rising in a skewed field.
The shape was historic and the hedge had
a wren in it; the slope had a rabbit
and the grass had a hare. The gate had a
chain on it, some bailing twine caught up in

it. Over the gate I go into the
memory, listing the proper names of
the places that knew you. Make me in metal
so that I may record them, Omey and
Ardmore, the back strand at Rossnowlagh.
Picture you swimming, mill pond always in
shadow, dark weedy water, the weed in
your hair. Abbey St Bathans and Broughton
and Fisherton, may all be recorded
this field in particular, the primrose

that's glinting so. Come by the copse, lay your
head by the primrose, read by the celandine's
light. Washed by the water, may your body
be perfumed by the bluebells that grow here.
sound of the swathy bee – see there's too little
Greek in me – hands that rework the history, place
your head by the primrose; you died here.

SUE LEIGH

Sue Leigh is a freelance editor living in the Cotswolds. She is working on her first collection of poetry while studying for a PhD at the University of Aberystwyth.

'Patterns', 'Coat' and 'September, 1940' were first published in *Oxford Magazine*.

My family history, like that of many of my generation, relates to the history of the two world wars. I wanted to write about it but I was all too aware of the difficulties. How could I write about something I hadn't known personally? Did I have any right to use the suffering of others as raw material? In choosing to write about the women left at home – knitting, gardening, writing letters and generally keeping the home fires burning – I was able to create a distance. And I hoped brevity would be a kind of tact, a respectful stepping back. Writing these poems made me realise that it's not the place of poetry to draw conclusions, make judgements or even to understand. All the poet can do is ask the reader to slow down, take stock, listen.

When my brother died I didn't know how to write about it. How could I write about an event that had turned my world upside down? How could I find a language for the unsayable? Instinctively, I turned to the natural world for some sort of consolation and I found the emotional vocabulary I needed for 'A sister's story' in a Hans Christian Andersen fairy tale, 'The Wild Swans'. These were short poems too. I wanted to approach the condition of silence, to leave imaginative space for the reader.

Where do my poems come from? Poems begin for me not with ideas but with a deep listening, like thinking with my whole body; attending to what Robert Frost called 'a tantalizing vagueness'. Usually a group of words or a phrase demands attention, like a branch tapping at the window. They hold the texture of the poem, like a seed, and that's how a poem begins if I am lucky. I always see a poem behind my eyes – a sunlit orchard, a lamplit cabin on a whaling ship, a Roma woman crouched by a fire – and the scene is set. The next part involves hard work, what is usually called 'craft'. I don't know where it's going to lead me – the end isn't always in sight when I begin – and the finished poem often surprises me.

I write because I love the tussle with language, the challenge of trying to create something rich and new. But poetry is not simply wordplay. It reflects something of the sensibility of the writer. It's a way of making sense of being in the world.

Patterns

All through the war you knitted,
socks and mufflers,
balaclavas,
gloves with no fingers,
your bone needles endlessly clicking
as if by keeping him warm
you could keep him safe.

Sitting by the lamp in the evening
counting the sage green rows,
you would think of women
working by rushlight
or the light of a single tallow candle
and how when it guttered out
they would knit on into the dark.

What I know about the Roma

just two words
their syllables unfamiliar on my tongue
lungo drom
the long road

that their history is as long as memory

that a woman must not comb her hair
in front of a man
nor pass in front of him
nor wash her clothes with his

that she is unclean
from the waist down
except to her husband
that she wears red at her wedding

that they will bury her standing

that she knows the future

that there is a roadside, a wagon under trees

cream and brown splashed ponies
are cropping at the grass
a lean dog circles a patch of ground

a woman crouches by a fire
watches her black pot boil

Letter to the Front

As I write, a sulphur-yellow butterfly
makes its unsteady journey across the grass.

On a still day I sowed parsnips
the fine dust of carrot seed.

I planted the early potatoes
just as you showed me

filling the trench with leaf mould
banking the earth up high.

Yesterday I found the first pale primroses
in the wood, the wild cherry is in flower

the ash waits for its leaves.

Coat

They sent it back.
Still the slight sourness of khaki
and fainter wet leaves,
woodsmoke.

In the pockets I felt
the rough raw edge of seam,
a small line of grit,
a tear in the lining.

We lay under it once.
I remember how we stayed awake
and watched the snow
falling endlessly into the night.

September, 1940

Years later she remembered that afternoon –
the bright clear light, the sharp shadows
the last of the swallows flying over the garden.

She had gone to the orchard to pick apples.
She heard the soft thud as the apples fell,
so many. They stared up from the grass.

Some split open in a fizz of juices,
wasps throbbed inside hollow windfalls.
Slowly the baskets filled. It was warm, still.

Just an ordinary day, an ordinary late summer day,
the last of the swallows flying over the garden –

he fell out of the sky while she was picking apples.

Scrimshaw

We sighted them two winters out of Nantucket
at daybreak

their backs
miraculous grey islands

we hunted the plumes of their breath

for three days the harpoon waved like a flag
from her head

the sea bled

and when we had finished the flensing
the scraping, the scooping

we boiled the oil

(which smelled so sweet and burned so bright
and was the colour of straw)

then I saved for myself
a milk-smooth tooth

scratched with my sail needle
a likeness of this sloop

and with lampblack
I darkened my name.

Cornfield

(after John Nash, 1918)

All day you draw from the wound of memory
the groaning silence, a mutilated wood

until your vision smudges in a blur of rain
your palette has no use for its colours

and you carry your easel out
to paint another field

harvest
the corn safely gathered in

the stooks orderly in their rows
casting such long shadows.

Poem for my brother

Each day visiting you I'd pass the blackthorn
unnoticed
until one of the last mornings of your life
when it seemed in the night
there had been a sudden late fall of snow.

A good tree for hedging you told me
you knew all those things
and that you should gather its fruit
after the first frosts
to make the drink tasting of almonds
we had each Christmas

but I had to tell you about
blackthorn winter –
the spell of cold that always follows the flower.

A sister's story

I remember a white ribbon of swans
flying low over water
my own silence

and the nettles
how could I forget the nettles
their stinging kiss

you could wear a swanshirt brother
as long as I knew sometimes you'd land
and glide over the water

to meet my outstretched hand.

Elegy

My words dissolve in salt
so I ask the wild geese
to fill the evening sky
again with their streamers
to call your name over
and over the marshes.

Look how they find their way back
to this place of water
light
to rest in this same small field
close to the sound of the sea.

OLIVIA McCANNON

Olivia McCannon has lived in Paris for eight years and is currently translating a new version of Balzac's *Old Goriot* for Penguin Classics. Her writing has appeared in various publications and on Radios 3 and 4. She received a Hawthornden Fellowship in 2005.

'Dust' was first published in *Modern Poetry in Translation*, 'Liverpool Echo' in *Saw*, 'Unborn' and 'Cohabitation' in *The Wolf*, 'Probability' in *Oxford Magazine* and then in *Penguin's Poems for Life* (2007). 'Mirror' came joint second in the Keats–Shelley Award and was published in the *Keats–Shelley Review*, then in *Modern Poetry in Translation*.

Poetry, for me, is a place where words can mean what they say. If I didn't believe this with all my heart, I wouldn't be able to write a word.

I used to feel overwhelmed by the ballast attached to my mother tongue. But for the past eight years, French has been my language of everyday communication, and as English has come to feel more foreign, writing in it has become simpler. David Constantine has said that 'the language of poetry should always carry with it some feeling of "coming from abroad"'. In my case, the sense of strangeness and possibility offered by the physical experience of this feeling has been salutary.

I have also come to feel most at home on borders: vast and complex territories rather than thin black lines. The terrain of translation is perhaps like a mountain range which, on a map, seems clearly defined and manageable, but once you are in it, overpowers you with its expanding scale and unknowability. Initially, you pass into the landscape, but over time, the landscape passes into you. Translation and poetry ask for a similar displacement of the self into the language.

Many of the voices in these poems were ones I wanted to hear in the flesh, but couldn't, for different reasons. I found words for them to speak, not to replace their own, but because I couldn't bear their silence. Although individual lines may be driven by the patterns of speech, I wrote these poems in the mode of song. The same physical sensation as that of being moved to sing – along with the extra effort and attention that singing and listening require – were conditions of their writing.

Bernard O'Donoghue: 'Poetry, like traditional music, is a product of, and a repayment to, community.' If I write at all, it is to be part of this quickening exchange.

Probability

He always tried to make it better
Put it right
To stop it happening at all was best.

Crossing the road he held her small hand
So tightly
Her knuckles turned white with his stress.

On cliff walks he kept her pressed right in
On the inside
Once she walked through a wasps' nest.

Once she jumped out of an upstairs window
She was fine
She wanted to see what can happen.

Number Ten

Into Number Ten they poured
The past, the present and the future
Held in the space between four walls.

The past tied up in the deposit
The present in the sum paid out each week
The future in someone else's pocket.

They owned the same rooms as next door
Walls that stayed lean even in fatter times
Windows too stiff to open for new air.

Hope went into flowers that outgrew borders
Ambition into the hammering in the shed
Happiness into gaps so small it had to bow its head.

Liverpool Echo

He's not there anymore, the man outside Marks and Sparks
Twice a minute every day for years, he shouted – *Cho!*

It was always winter and always dark
His – *Cho!* was church-loud, hollow and cold.

A blast of mist, shaped by his mouth's warm hole
Into an O as irrevocable as crematorium smoke.

Wiping out the *Socks and Lighters three for a pound Ladies*
As it hacked across the drawn strings of his throat.

A relentless prophet in a worn-thin donkey jacket
His cover was the smudgy newspaper he sold.

Let someone draw his outline on the brick in chalk
His silence, like his noise was, is that hole

When twilight traced around the skyline
When the lit-up tower restaurant was a place you'd never go,

While on the Mersey, ships arrived and left as shadows
And foghorns joined their gloom to his – *Cho!*

While flurries of starlings kept breaking up the dark –
Singing particle swarms, black hearts numb with cold –

He was always there, the man outside Marks and Sparks
Twice a minute every day for years, he shouted – *Cho!*

Unborn

Once you were a frozen dead girl
I rescued from a lake too late.
I zipped you into my jacket and held you
Against me for hours until I felt
Your warm breath moisten the air again.
We walked into the city –
So many people. But couldn't
Find your parents anywhere.

Another time I had you on a cushion
Under a shawl in a shopping basket,
Birth presents tucked around you.
We were both younger then.
I raised the blanket to watch you as you slept
And underneath were hard-limbed plastic dolls
With glossy eye-whites and shellac lashes
Staring at the sky behind my back.

Paper Tiger

I queued for three years in the rain outside your door
Shuffling in slippers between barriers, head bowed

To deflect the glare of your guns and windows
Carefully holding the pink and green slips of paper,

The specially sized photos that were asked for
With a centimetre's length between nose and chin.

My face had washed away, my name dissolved
By the time my number showed and you let me in.

Dust

Most of my life is buried in that room.
I look in through the shattered glass

And see a conversation strobed
Out by the blast. I ran across

This continent so that the dust,
Which fell for years, could not bury the rest.

Cohabitation

Sometimes it was a bombed-out house
Carpeted with the shards of a meagre life
That the family would walk over with bare feet
Pretending, for the child, to find something to eat,

Or an exterminating wind or wall of water
Crushing bodies into its bricks and mortar,
Or an eye lined with sticky black flies
And a hand too limp to flick them away,

Or the hardened voice, the scarred face
Of a dazed child trailing a sad stump –
Which drove them to the plot of wasteland
That used to be our rubbish dump.

We stare at them through bullet-proof glass.
Often they just blur into the background
Until a pillar of smoke, a blast of firecrackers
Remind us we live next to the favela.

City of the Dead (Cairo)

I live in the shadow of the Sultan's tomb,
He lies in my light. I listen, at dawn
For the voices of his retinue, but
Mum says they spoke louder with their eyes.

No matter – the sitcoms start at nine.
We've got a dish up by the dome
To fish out voices from the ether
Faces from other worlds and eras.

Dad says we wear the masks of the dead
Their blood runs through our veins
Their thoughts run through our heads.
We are invisible, like them.

Tourists don't find us picturesque
Postmen can't find the numberless,
Addresses here are arabesques
And so we live between the lines

Of tombs and sleep on stone and bones
With wives and slaves and dancers.
No big deal. Sultan's pleasure.
We breathe the air that they do not –

Desert air. Infused with drying dust.
It would be clean as death itself
Without us Living with our flesh
Our fumes, our faeces, and our food.

Mirror

I've got a mirror hanging from my pack
It stares up at the sky. The sky stares back.

The pretty half of my mum's powder compact
We left the rest in a heap, ten miles back.

All gone, the powder that kept her young
Daily facemasks of dust have made us old.

The only thing still pink is my dry tongue
Poking the cavities filled with our last gold.

I can never see more than a piece of my face
Never more than an eye and half a nose.

We've been walking through this waste for days
Wearing the same black as our shadows.

Dad says it must be 40 in the shade.
And no shade anywhere. Walking for days

For days and our bones are dryer than ever,
We skitter like dead leaves across the map.

With all this light we're lighter now than ever
Our packs emptier but heavier now than ever

Every day it is even harder than ever
To open our eyes and let the sand pour in.

Today I stared so hard at the sky it cracked.

HILARY MENOS

Hilary Menos was born in Luton in 1964. She studied PPE at Wadham College, Oxford, then worked in journalism. Her pamphlet *Extra Maths* is published by Smith/Doorstop Books, and her first collection will be published by Seren in 2008/9. She runs an organic farm in Devon with her partner and four children.

'Extra Maths' was first published in *Smiths Knoll* 30, 'Cluedo' in *Envoi* 138 under the title 'Architect', and 'Gift' was first published in *Magma* 31. 'Face of America' won the *Envoi* International Poetry Competition 2002.

As to 'why poetry', I can think of three possible reasons. My mother read me poetry as a child – Walter de la Mare, T.S. Eliot, Dylan Thomas – and made reel-to-reel tapes for me to listen to as I fell asleep. My father spent hours every night drafting and redrafting technical documents, publicity material, minutes of meetings – I almost never saw him without an A4 pad and a stubby pencil and he would worry for hours over the meaning, and placement, of one word. And when I left my junior school at eleven, Mr Sutcliffe told me never to stop writing poetry. We all have a Mr Sutcliffe. I have a photo of Mr Sutcliffe probably taken in 1975, now looking absurdly old-fashioned, and somewhere I still have my Bushmead Junior School poetry writing book, a thin exercise book which was, I now realise, the same shade of orange as I picked out for the cover of my pamphlet *Extra Maths*.

I hope my poetry is fairly firmly rooted in the real. I co-run a 75-acre mixed organic farm in Devon, and often write about nature and traditional rural life, but not, I hope, in a prissy or romanticised way – no herons, no buttercups, no fluffy lambs – I'm more of a slaughterhouse and slurry pit poet. Another inspiration for me to write is global environmental damage, but I'd hate to be thought of as a tub-thumper. I like my poems to be oblique, though not obscure, and not political except in the broader sense. Beyond this, I write about all sorts of stuff – my three most recent poems are about Bernard Manning, going to the dentist, and the 1960s cult movie *Fantastic Voyage*. Although they are really about community, death, and our misplaced trust in science. And, of course, whatever you as a reader bring.

Finally, there are lots of different ways to say something and poets might as well say it in as interesting and entertaining a way as possible. And, generally, brevity is a good thing.

Extra Maths

My father is giving me extra maths. I am ten.
If one tap fills the bath at the rate of a litre a minute
and one fills the bath at the rate of a gallon an hour
and water escapes from the plughole at two pints a second
how long before we can take a bath?

I stand on one leg. My brother is watching TV.
Outside the other kids are bombing the hill on a go-kart.
My father gouges his pipe with his penknife,
dumping black tar into his cold baked beans.
My mother hates it.

Upstairs, water seeps over the rolled enamel rim,
steals down the side of the bath and through the boards,
easing its way down the white plastic flex
of the light fitting over my father's head
at a rate incalculable to man.

Face of America

They had to sew her into the dress it was that tight,
tighter than a mermaid's skin and shimmered like scales.
Mother of God! You could see it in their eyes –
a hunger for what she'd got. Nobody knows
how she did it, but she looked for all the world
like someone who'd got all the answers. The big 'Yes'.

Every now and then beauty steps forward.
On a shell, a chariot, a podium. Rolled up in a rug.
And for one brief moment time itself steps back.
Then there's the fall, the war, the telephone call,
the men in suits with white powder, dusting for prints
and, up on a billboard, the face of America, smiling.

Neighbours

Stonechats chip and bounce above the hedge,
and swifts surf the breeze, their forked tails
flicking the vees, but this is not what we're here for.
Here comes Bob with his dogs. One barks, one bites.

John has the farm in the valley, peppercorn rent
but he's broke. Down a potholed track, old man Tucker
hawks and spits at crows. His bungalow lurks
by the barn. Sunset flushes the slurry gold.

When the wind is right we hear Mick shooting rats
and Kate screaming Stop, then just screaming.
She won't last long. There's a witch at Druid's Cross
– we keep our kids inside on ancient days.

Through the blue haze specked with long-leg flies I see Bob
tying baler twine round the neck of the one that barks.

Faithless

I knew him by his hair, more Gabriel
than Gabriel himself. And how sparks flew.
We went to it like wayward souls, him
shoved against the wall, shirt off,
poised for flight, knowing, like a sepia-tint
street-girl, debauched and glowing. I traced
the scalloped scars that straddled his spine.
Faithless. I made him mine.

At once the excuses: the distance, the cost.
When he said he was leaving I knew this a lesson
I'd already learnt. Once bitten, twice burnt.
Both blessed and cursed. Both lost.
Now nights are loose and strange. I deal in never,
but dream of an angel's rub and rush of feathers.

Floorboards

Floorboards, she said, with that typically French shrug
straight from Napoleon via Charles de Gaulle.
So all that summer we tiptoed round the flat
knowing Cecile was down there, being quiet.

Stairs were the worst, and August. We pissed in bowls,
refused to take the three steps down to the loo.
We slept on the living room floor, watched silent films,
ate cornflakes and cheap jam, whispered

about boundaries, how to manage the space
between people – that line of my father's – how
my right to swing my arm stops at your nose.
And underneath each stifled creak, Cecile.

We bought the screws, borrowed a friend's drill
but it was always too hot, or too early, or too late.
The ants were swarming. Sometimes Cecile played music,
its muffled drumbeat nudging our consciences.

Until we saw her load the van – eiderdowns,
a kettle trailing its flex – and watched her drive away.
We pulled the carpets up that night, screwed
down the boards. Days later, you went, too.

Mistress

Polish Anna writes: 'Please let me know
where you laid him to rest, finally.'
She wants to pay her respects to a handful of ash
buried under the spread of the apple tree
in the garden of the house where I was born,

in a hole barely a spade's width, spade's depth,
and me concerned about speeches, and dogs,
then picking flowers and balancing them
on a mound that looks less like a burial site
and more like a small repair in Astroturf.

I carry his empty box back in, jangling
four screws in my pocket, knowing the house
would be sold, and him with it, still not sure
if that was the best place for him, wondering what
you and all the others would have done.

So I put off writing back to you, in your tiny
Warsaw flat, partly to preserve the equilibrium
of new owners, Mr and Mrs Patel, but more,
because I do not really know where
or indeed if I have laid him to rest, finally.

Cluedo

He has mapped our future in black ink
on three sheets of paper. He unfolds them,
spreads them on the table in the pub,
smoothing them with hands that draw
a perfect circle, perfect straight line.

Our house rises to greet us, north elevation,
then hunkers down among the bunched contours
of the land survey. He plots parking,
a gravel drive, a porch to shelter friends
as they wait, clutching Chardonnay, flowers.

The plans are detailed minutely, each stone
hand drawn. So clear I can see myself dust.
My profile in the kitchen making jam,
you washing the car, our outline children
playing, picking apples, riding bikes.

Gift

I want to write you a small square poem
that starts with space and a vague notion of form
then pitches in headlong – not holding its nose
at the pull of another body – to atmosphere,
the curve of coastline, a fjord's fold and wrinkle,
borders, boundaries, the abrupt hyphenation of dams,
and hurtles through the sprawl of domes and spires
of a small Italian town to a piazza where,
between candy-stripe carts of ice-cream sellers,
past lunchtime chatter, waiters bringing Lavazza
and orange juice, it finds firm ground,
lands on the page like a flag, like a map of a world
impossible to resist and, catching the wind,
unfurls and soars like a bird circling the square.

MIRIAM OBREY

Miriam Obrey lives in Shropshire and works as a counsellor in GP surgeries. She has led writing workshops through the Poetry Society's Poetry Placements Scheme and Warwick University's Advanced Writing Programme. Her poems have been widely anthologised and her pamphlet *A Case for More Heads* was published by Flarestack in 1996.

'The Bullet' won second prize in the Ledbury Poetry Competition in 2003; 'The Walking Years' won first prize in the same competition in 1999. 'Harry' and 'Goldfinch' were first published in the Arvon International Poetry Competition anthology in 2004, 'The Afterlife of a Wedding Dress' was first published in the Essex Poetry Festival 2003 competition winners' anthology, and 'Disembodied' was first published by *Thumbscrew*.

Many of my poems are sparked by memory – of my father, his stories, and lessons on the natural world. 'The Bullet' and 'The Walking Yews', with their strange and diverse imagery, draw also on a powerful sense of place, myth and local history.

The poem 'Disembodied' was partly inspired by the paintings *Death and Life*, (1911–16) and *Virgin* (1913) by Gustav Klimt; by war, death-pits and also my interest in change, the hope of renewal and metamorphosis. 'Resurrection' was directly inspired by Stanley Spencer's studies made in Cookham, especially his painting *Swan Upping at Cookham* and his *Resurrection, Cookham* (1924–6).

The title 'Bagging Daylight' came out of a snatch of overheard conversation. It was used to describe the monotonous and mundane experienced by a person in the course of his work. Here, borrowing a technique from Browning, I have juxtaposed unrelated imagery and ideas which have merged to create a surreal mindscape in which the negative, if not transformed by the positive, shifts towards a sense of hope in its changing perspective.

In my gap year I worked in a forestry nursery alongside an octogenarian who told me about the local ways and customs that coloured his life. My interest in Worcestershire, its idiom and folklore stems from this time and has been a passion ever since. The poem 'Harry' is darkly inspired by my memories of him and his wife, of local footpaths – his naming of fields and copses – a changing landscape and a lost way of life.

My discovery of letters, diaries, and other family records prompted 'The Afterlife of a Wedding Dress'. It is written in the imagined voice of my great-grandmother after she fled America during the civil wars and thereafter became deeply unhappy, isolated from friends and family, cooped up in Worcestershire in a loveless marriage.

Continuing my themes of loss, hope and renewal: after learning how Osip Mandelstam's poems survived his incarceration and death – how they were first consigned to memory by him, then by his wife, friends and fellow prisoners – my poem 'Goldfinch' came so spontaneously it felt like a gift that had written itself.

The Bullet

A centimetre more and it would have torn
through my grandfather's lungs,
stopping his heart

as the chocolate in his ration box stopped the bullet.
My father and I, my children and theirs,
would have been breath

condensing on a dead soldier's lips. A widow's fiction.
I used to wonder what it tasted like, the chocolate,
three melded slabs of it

never touched by man or mouse
as it lay in its box through a second war
when my father choreographed his hat trick.

A hip full of shrapnel. His rip cord stuck.
His fall broken by a tree
and I think of us numbered among its acorns.

The Walking Yews

When I was eight my father taught me
to cross the road at Dick Brook bridge
to set crayfish traps, to tickle trout
and how to tell pedunculate from sessile oak.

Later, he taught me to suck flesh
from the pit of a yew berry,
to spit out seed which, swallowed
he said, would kill me

as sure as it would pass intact
through a mistle thrush,
that its green and bitter sap
would drag me underground;

that I would drown
where Dick Brook met the River Styx
and join the sixpence I swallowed
in the last year's Christmas pudding.

I survived his lessons
like the DNA of Viking kings
whose burial mounds against the sky
were crowned with yews –

ancestors of trees that have walked
through leaf-mould and clay,
following tracks and bridle-paths
from its crest, to mark a boundary

between the foot of Ramscombe hill
and the field
where old man Rea grazes his Friesians.

Harry

His boot prints forged a path
below the rookery in Darling's Grove
past Hanging Hollow

a copse whose history is dark
as a nest of baby rooks
bagged and feathered by firelight,

dark as slag lugged home from Astley,
sacks of small coal shedding dust
through a backyard into his kitchen,

enough to blacken the cheek of an angel:
Harry's goodwife Alice –
could be mother earth herself

slumped in a greenwood rocker –
one tooth and few words left
to show for fifty seasons spent

topping carrots
in ten degrees or more of frost
that has turned her breath into a halo,

docking frozen swedes without gloves
Harry says
her hands warm as two pups in his.

The Afterlife of a Wedding Dress

I've slung my veil between the legs
of an upturned chair and filled it with blackberries.
I've squared my muslin petticoats for dusters.
Out of the ivory skirt, I've cut and sewn
a frock for our daughter and rompers for our son.
I'm feeding them muffins and bramble jelly
that drips through the veil. Blackberries
have left a map of America on its netting –
if I half close my eyes I can just see Natchez
and the yard where I played with my toys
and my goats in the Mississippi sun.
I've made Plasticine animals for the children.
Two elephants
to float across the bath in a white satin slipper.

And if one becomes a boat for elephants,
the other slipper could be a measure for corn.
A scoop for feeding the birds. A pot
for a posy of poppies or forget-me-nots,
its toe a refuge for wasps to winter
nine dark foggy months.
Time in which to carry your child.
Time to wait for the wild geraniums –
that first wet feeding place for fledgling wrens.

The joy of eyebright and scarlet pimpernel.
The whirr of swifts as they wing down
under the eaves sacrificing their summer
to the next generation. Or, that other slipper
my love, could be a coffin for a chick.

Bagging Daylight

...so I sat her down like Alice in front of a mirror.
She stared out through the mist of it and said:
look at what is not for me and where I've never been:
I've never seen rainbows in the eyes of a grieving mother;
I've never breathed a word of her language – Muerto –
'give me back, give him back, give her back'.
I've never walked that tightrope across the sea
nor felt the impress of its braided hemp on the soles of my feet.
I've never walked the streets with nothing
but holes in my pockets. Hell –
I've never felt the puppet strings of that.
I've never slipped and fallen in a hall of marbles.

Oh, I said, *you've been bagging daylight*
in the smallest of rooms
full of red, yellow, blue and green
balloons full of someone else's breath
where you have drowned and yet,
you tell me you've heard music made by rain
seeping in through a hole in the roof;
that you understand its random notes;
that you have cupped a hatching egg in your hand
and here, with your feet on the ground
and your head in a cloud, you tell me
you have seen the moon in the eye of a toad.

Goldfinch

in memory of Osip Mandelstam

A bird swept out of its element
somewhere among the blackthorn
whose twigs clench buds like pearl fists.
Blink and you'll miss it: the hawk
that grounded the goldfinch

leaving a circle of feathers –
yellow, red. Shades
that exist in a handful of soil.
Colour that has no name
mussed by a draught in the grass.

The finch, mute but for the charm
passing its voice
from one bird to the next
from thicket to copse,
its liquid gold suspended in an egg.

Disembodied

She closed butterfly eyelids
as she reached for my hand
in the morning's first light
that melted fabric into flowers.

As she reached for my hand
among right-angled limbs
fabric melted into flowers
taking root in a pit.

Among right-angled limbs,
my sisters, forever young,
taking root in a pit,
tangle with algae and marigolds.

My sisters, forever young,
hug each other – as their days
tangle with algae and marigolds
linden, indigo and violet,

hug each other as their days
open butterfly eyelids –
linden, indigo and violet –
in the morning's first light.

Resurrection

after Stanley Spencer's Resurrection

All those swans from *Swan Upping*
getting muddled up with it – the second coming.
Jesus in a boat. Fathers, sons and grandfathers
crawling like anaemic earwigs
from under the lids of coffins and tombs.
Cookham in bloom. Its dogs and cats
looking for a scrap. The last call.
Trumpeters. An angel host
rising from the golden section: fishwives
and midwives. Goodwives, mothers and their daughters.
Toddlers, babies, twins. A glorious resurrection
stretching beyond the rainbow and, caught
among its brushstrokes, Stanley himself
in his wild pastiche of flesh and apple blossom.

JO ROACH

Jo Roach was born and brought up in London where she still lives. Her father was from Ireland. She has been published in many magazines, including *Poetry London*, *Poetry Wales*, *Pen International*, *Cimarron Review* (USA) and *The Stony Thursday Book* (Ireland). Her pamphlet *Dancing at the Crossroads* was published by Hearing Eye in 2003.

'Saying Goodbye', 'St Patrick's Day Poem' and 'The Silver Trophy' were first published in the Poetry School anthology *Entering The Tapestry* (Enitharmon 2003). 'On Not Receiving a Vocation' and ' Firstborn' were first published in *The Stony Thursday Book*, 'Bread and Butter' was first published in *Cimarron Review*, 'At my Mother's Funeral' in *Redbrick Review*, and 'Ghost in the Machine' in *Poetry Wales* and the anthology *In the Company of Poets* (Hearing Eye 2003).

Author photograph reproduced by permission of Sylvie Edge.

The only process common to all my poems is that I do a lot of cleaning and tidying up before I begin. Perhaps, as with a poem when we focus on the detail, I should best describe how I came to write one poem in particular. After the shock of the stillbirth of my first baby, I searched for poems that could express my feelings and that I could hold physically – I found 'For A Child Born Dead' by Elizabeth Jennings, an elegy full of acceptance, ending with, 'Then all our consolation is / That grief can be as pure as this'.

Many years later, when I started to read and write poetry myself, Pascale Petit suggested that if you want to write about a difficult subject, first explore animal behaviour. I read *Moortown Diary* by Ted Hughes, in particular his poem 'Struggle', on the death of a stillborn calf and I was very struck by the line 'So she could get to know him with lickings'. I wrote my poem 'Firstborn' as a response, thinking 'if only human grief were so short lived'.

I write about the everyday as though I'm in conversation with a particular poem or with a person. I began writing after a hospital visit for tests. There was a woman in the waiting room who made us all laugh, saying, 'You'll never guess what the nurse asked me. She asked me if I'm on the Pill. I said, what, me at 69, I should be so lucky.' When I went for my test she touched me on the arm and said in her lovely Cockney accent, 'You'll be alright love.' I was so moved by the woman that I wrote about her. The writing came out in the shape of a poem, so I joined a creative writing class to find out if it was. And I've been writing ever since.

On Not Receiving a Vocation

How I pray not to be chosen to have my head shaved,
take a bath in my underwear and be silent.
I am not worthy to be burnt at the stake
or crushed on a wheel. Let it be Billy Mullins,
whose head seems too heavy for his neck,
who never catches the girls at kiss chase.
Please take him as thy servant.
Lord I am not worthy, since I pushed him off his chair
for sitting beside me in needlework.
The needle infected his hand for weeks,
the class chanted that his hand would have to be amputated.
Billy's scar – his stigmata, singles him out
for Holy Orders. Lord have mercy.

Bread and Butter

I come from women called Mrs Ashforth, Mrs Draper,
broken biscuits, cracked eggs, Co-op divi, provident cheques,
bomb ruins, Tin Tan Tommy,
a longing for an older brother's Gresham Flyer,
from Dolly Wheeler wearing her apron
in a photo of the Coronation party.

I come from looney bins and whalebone corsets,
hysterectomies, the change, varicose veins.
I come from Parky riding his bike
to lock the gates for the night,
a waltz at the bandstand,
reading the tea leaves,
the bearded lady at the fairground.

I come from the kitchens of women,
owners of preserving pans and garden fences.
I come from land lost in a hand of cards.
I come from girls who had no schooling.
I come from the deaths of Holy Martyrs.
I come from women married to men
who laboured in a country they didn't call home.

Ghost in the Machine

Jack Davis in overalls, wearing a cap
after his day job as a brickie, repairs
secondhand bikes, to earn extra
to pay the mortgage on the house he painted
green, white and yellow, at the time of ads
in corner shops, Rooms to let, no blacks no irish.

In the box room of number 16, spare wheels
hang from six-inch nails, the floor a shingle
of nuts and bolts, the smell of three-in-one oil
heavy as khaki. Hands fretted from wire wool
he polishes aluminium rims to silver, removes
links from the chain until it fits.

His memory full of the sea,
fine tunes into each wave
as if it were the one that broke when he left
a country where there are no words for yes and no.
Sue-Sue Lambert shopping in Dunlaoghaire
meets one of the Davises and asks,
Is Jack not after coming home?

Saying Goodbye

On the doorstep, with
an armful of milk bottles,
rinsed clean for the morning,
I see the doctor out: Dr Dalton
who wears a suit that doesn't fit,
the black frames of his glasses
hide his eyes, he's not a handsome man.
I ask, 'When is she going to get better?'
He doesn't lie and I thank him,
still holding the bottles.

At my Mother's Funeral

I watch my father for signs, as if
checking for the rash of a disease,
but his suit is buttoned-black,
the careful knot in his tie, you could see
a face in his shoes. We drink whisky
out of glasses too good to use and eat
thin slices of ham on-the-bone in our front room
with her sister Rosie who's the spit.
Out come the photos, the holiday at Butlins,
my mother in a halter-neck and pencil skirt
shoulders bare, hair blown back.
Then I see too much of him wanting
her to walk in and say put the glasses away
we're saving them for best.

Comfort

There's been nothing but rain for days now,
the house is full of wet washing.
It could be my mother's kitchen,
the clothes-horse in front of the range
and she's there taking a light from a coal,
a cow's lick of nicotine on her white hair.

On days such as these that soak to the skin
I am the girl under the table
while my mother hides the knives,
counts the seconds between thunder claps
and when the storm has passed
there's the smell of her lighting up again.

Woman to Woman

She spoke in a low voice,
as though down on her knees
in the dark-cornered confessional,
about the electric shock treatment,
the heavy sedation
that made her tongue swell
leaving her mute for a time,
the rubber soles of nurses' shoes
squeaking on the polished linoleum.
Although on most days my mother
played the piano with a light touch
her patient fingers filling our house with music,
there were times when I caught the look,
the look of stone in her grey eyes.

Stars Unfurl

Sally cries in her sleep and the foetus stirs
in its own small dark. We're all expecting
summer babies each one from the heart of a dying star.
During the consultant's morning round
the damp haired girl turns her head away
she is desperate for a boy.
Carnations crammed in a Nescafé jar
on the bedside locker. A dish of sugared almonds
an open card that the curtains flick over. We scan
the sky for the origin of meteors, to learn
how the night was made.
Down in the square, Carol in her nightdress
listens to the fountain.
The Summer Triangle is easily seen with the naked eye.
Emmie is sure she'll have a girl
since she dangled her wedding ring on a string
and watched its clockwise spin,
she reads our horoscopes out loud.
In the day room we crowd around the telly
as Neil Armstrong walks on the moon,
together we cheer him on and hold our sunrise bellies.

Possibilities of Blue

I spent the first few weeks of my daughter's life
looking into her eyes wondering at the possibility
of them remaining blue.

I watch brick bees in my garden
make small journeys between the thistles,
take satisfaction in naming the bees.

I catch sight of pond skaters,
quick darts on the surface of deep water
then something joyful in a duet of cabbage whites
and I hear the paediatrician say
'She's charming, one of those children
with a butterfly mind.'

I notice the transitory electric of a damselfly.

There is no name for her disability,
no label to understand her by,
nothing to pin her down.

Designed for small birds, my new bird feeder
offers protection from those more able
to take care of themselves
with their red and gold voices.

My daughter of chance disability
changes the word order
when she writes, 'Suzie from love'.
How I rely on those words to keep her safe.

My daughter's eyes

What I wish for her
are things I cannot give
this adult child of mine.
Once when she was late
home in the dark
I saw her face
on every girl
with silky hair falling
in a straight bob.
My daughter's eyes
are the same as mine
when she cries,
to comfort myself
I want to teach her
how to live without me.

For my Daughter

And you Suzie, what should I leave you?
Not the pewter statue of the boy
his right hand missing,
let him stay on the mantelpiece
for the second-hand dealers.
Not photos of my mother who died
before you were born into that grieving time.
Not money, to be banked for you
by someone else.
Not my poems, you'll never read them.
But the very fiercest of watchdogs
who wouldn't sleep for a hundred years.

Firstborn

If you had been a calf
I would have coaxed you
with warm wet tongue slaps,
licking off the vernix
from your eyes mouth nostrils,
sure of your smell
and when you didn't breathe
known when to walk away.

St Patrick's Day Poem

If you paint Roseanna's portrait
put weight on her
as though she'd often eaten
soda bread with buttermilk.
Stroke a blush on her cheeks
as if she were breathless from dancing
up at the Ballybrack crossroads.
Whiten her hands, straighten her back.
Leave out the lines on her face
and that pained look in her eyes,
dark as a priest's soutane.
Keep the wedding ring
out of the picture.
Put a shine on her black hair
as though I had brushed it.

The Silver Trophy

His nicotined fingers tie fishing flies
of teal feather and rabbit fur,
his calloused palm dirty against
the glint of the metal hook.
He arcs the line across the lake
and waits. Rolls his own in one hand,
draws the paper over his tongue
with just enough spit to hold the edge.
Later at the sound of him
coming in through the door, didn't Annie
and the young one, their eyes lowered,
lift the table and put it down
in front of him. Him with not one word
to say to those children of his, as he
cleared his plate, then set to;
to gut the fish into a bucket,
swilling his hands in the bloodied water.
I remember nothing of his dying, only
the darkness of Glendalough and him fishing there.

ANNA ROBINSON

Anna Robinson was the first recipient of the Poetry School Schol-
arship. Her first publication is *Songs from the Flats* (Hearing Eye
2005). Set on a housing estate in South London, it explores themes
of home and rebellion within an urban dream-time. It was the
Poetry Book Society pamphlet choice for winter 2005/6.

The inspiration point of a poem is, and should be, mysterious. However, the writing process, in its wider sense (drafting, editing) is something I have wanted to understand more fully in recent years.

Formally, I like to keep things open, so that I don't limit the possibilities of a poem too early on. But, I have a need to learn, during the writing process, what it is that I mean. I set out to find what my poetic discourse might be. In 2002, I enrolled for an MA in Public History at Ruskin College, Oxford. Taught by Hilda Kean and Paul Martin, Public History encourages a fierce questioning of the way we perceive history in all its forms: academic, 'heritage', nostalgia, mythic and popular. I found this useful in beginning to understand what I seem to want to say and it also equipped me to 'play' a bit with how I do that.

I'm thrilled with the editors' selection. The poems are quite different from each other, which might make them seem an odd choice collectively, but they all represent turning points for me.

The estate I live on celebrated its hundredth anniversary in 2001, and most of the quotes in 'The Flats' came from things people told me whilst I was collecting stories for a community history. This was the poem in which I began to get closer to tapping into a particular voice (one of my own many voices) that was proving harder to write than my normal 'poetry voice'; harder because it is less formally educated and less heard in poetry.

'Portraits of Women' was a response to finding that, despite the way society has changed, Jack the Ripper's victims are still regarded, at least by published 'Ripperologists', as dehumanised corpses! I found records at the National Archives; testimonies from friends of the women. These are the words of people in shock and already myth-making, the way we do when people die. Not the stuff of essays; not without lots of extra research and theoretical commentary and all I'd wanted to say was 'look – they were real and were once alive!' It was during a prose poetry course, at the Poetry School, that I realised this was the form in which to let the material and my own projections do their thing. The non-linear nature of prose poetry suited the apparent randomness of the narratives.

The Flats

The cats know their lands, which bit of yard
is theirs, and the lie of corridors, across
shed roofs where they can freely pass

down by the back of the rec., and I know mine.
My corners are the nettle patch and by
the bins, our common ground the washing line.

My neighbour said in those days we never
had kitchens, we'd cook everything on the range.
The ghost of my hearth has moved next door,

I can hear her playing that trumpet into the night.
My neighbour said in those days you couldn't
afford holidays. My neighbour sleepwalks, but not

in the back yard, that's mostly my patch. She walks
round her bedroom, down the hallway, feeling,
looking for that fifth room, the one without a door.

My neighbour said the caretakers used to decorate
your indoors. They had a book with three sorts
of wallpaper. If we neighbours see each other

in the street we say Oo-oo! and flick a hand
as if we were dancing – or waiting to –
sometimes we only mouth it – but still we dance.

My neighbour said Monday mornings down here,
women used to come out with prams loaded
with stuff: suits, watch-chains, whatever,

and go down the pawn shop – it was the norm.
Years ago, said my neighbour, you never
had mains electricity. My neighbour's door

is black, like mine. My neighbour gave me a recipe:
'Where the bread though stale is in good shape,
butter and make sandwiches with left over meat.

Beat an egg, dip and fry in good lard, send
to the table with lettuce and watercress.'
My neighbour, who shall remain nameless, said

Don't tell no one but there was once a man
whose sister lived down here, and he was killed;
and how they done it was they'd held him down

and made him swallow the bracelet that he'd bought
his lady-friend. Choked him. He didn't know,
but she was married and her husband was not

the sort you cross. In those days you could leave
your door unlocked. We've got wildlife in our yard,
self-seeding, wind-loving but we also have pansies.

He let himself in, said my neighbour,
and there on the table was a dinner plate
on it was kippers and he said, Oh no

not bleedin' kippers again – and then
the neighbour came through and said, 'Sod off
to your own bleedin' flat!' See, in them

days all the keys was the same – all the doors –
there was only one lock, it wasn't his dinner.
My neighbour was telling me all about the war.

It has rained for three days, the yard is empty
except for us, some snails and the pansies.
My neighbour says I could murder a cup of tea.

The Breath of Elephants

You know those times
when a man won't do,
not even a big man
in fireman's uniform
and your sleep is fitful?

That's when you dream of elephants.
Big herds that stand
round, sniff you out
and if they like you,
which they always do, in dreams,

flap their ears and tell you
in low rumblings that you may
sniff back. They smell of wood
and salt, their breath smells
of wet leaves. You reach

out to stroke a trunk,
which is rough except after rain
when the velvet stands proud.
They feel you back,
run fingery trunk ends

down your arm, exploring
your useless skin,
too soft for real weather,
then gently they lean.
You have won their approval.

The matriarch steps forward,
wraps her trunk tight
around your waist and lifts
you high. The Sun bursts,
you're bathed in light.

Portraits Of Women – East London – 1888

Mary Ann (Polly) Nicholls

The locksmith's daughter has a heart-shaped face. Her chestnut hair is pinned back, in the style we all wear. Her fringe is two curls, which fall half way down her forehead. Her eyebrows are comet shaped. Her lips are full but not wide and she likes a gin. Her eyes are grey. She keeps her things neat and tonight she has a new black bonnet made of straw and trimmed with velvet. The docks are on fire; the flames have turned the sky red. We can see this from the pub. Her nose is small. Her feet are small. She doesn't mind the shadows thrown from Buck's Row. She'll find her doss. She'll be back in a minute. Keep the bed warm.

Annie Chapman

Her movements are, eventually, always easterly. Steady, sturdy, she walks, always circling that idea, with a good wide stride. Her face is round. Her eyes are blue. Her dark brown hair is curly. It holds pins tolerably. Her fringe is thick and long. Her lips are full. She is pale. She is dying and will do what she wants. Crochet, she loves to crochet – but where is the hook? She does not drink except for rum. She moves with the ghost of a young girl beside her. Her son is a cripple. Her daughter has run away to the circus. The fences along Hanbury Street are five feet tall. She is five feet tall. *See that Tim keeps the bed for me.* Twenty-nine is her favourite number. She always sleeps at number twenty-nine.

Elizabeth Stride

Tall, this one, and Swedish. She says her husband and children were killed in a steamboat crash, but that is a lie. Now, she is living with a waterman. Her jacket is fur trimmed. She has been eight times before the magistrate in twenty months. Her ears are elves' ears. Her eyes grey. Her long face ends in a neat bulbish chin. Her mouth is wide and held in a smile and her dark hair flicks in outward curls. She does not understand the Bible. We call her Long Liz. She has her doss. She earned it cleaning. She keeps a key in her petticoat pocket. It is for the padlock the waterman uses to try to make her stay.

Catherine Eddowes

The tin-plate worker's daughter has come south, from Wolver-
hampton. She has had her share of husbands, the gallows balladeer
(whose initials she has tattooed on her arm) and the lampblack
packer, and now she is with a fruit seller who has a dodgy cough.
They sleep at Cooney's lodgings and spend the summers hop
picking. She is short and slim with brown eyes and dark red hair.
She has been arrested for impersonating a fire-engine down
Aldgate. We all saw it happen. The fruit seller loves her; they have
never had a row despite her famous temper. She is an educated
woman. She wears no fringe; her eyebrows are owlish. She has
gone to find her daughter who has flown since last time and left
no forwarding address.

Mary Jane Kelly

She is Irish, this girl, but speaks fast, in Welsh. Big handed and tall,
she has thick blonde hair, with a fringe that flops long on one side.
Her eyes are blue. Her man is a porter at Billingsgate, or was. She
has been loved by many men and I am telling the truth: really
loved. Even by some who paid good money. I am truthful, as she
is, always, and that can be hard. Her song is 'A Violet from
Mother's Grave'. The flower seller hates it and cannot sleep. She
has a way of standing on the street, as if she were on a stage. Miller's
Court is her haven and where a girl in trouble can find her. 'The
Fisherman's Widow' adorns her fireplace wall. Her apron is
always spotlessly clean.

Odes 1.5

Who is this boy, wet with scent, slim and
pressing you into the rose bushes
    down by the smiling grotto, Pyrrha?
      Who do you pin your hair for

with such style? So, how many times
will he cry over your flexible faith
    and gods, and stare, amazed, as black
      winds create roughened water,

he who enjoys you, believes you gold,
forever available, forever worth loving,
    doesn't yet know the false breeze.
      Heartbroken – those for whom

untested you shine. The votive tablet
on the temple wall shows I have hung
    my wet clothes up to the god
      who is Lord of the Sea.

Horace – trans. Anna Robinson

Pyrrha's response

You are wrong, wet man, this boy
is sweet, he does not ask for gold
or 'forever' he wants nothing
but what is found in the roses.

I did my best, wet man, your wet
god knows I did, but on our last
night I slept and dreamt I was cat.
I was wild, fierce, full of

spit and squall, and a fear in me
so huge it became my body.
When I woke my clothes were soaked.
So, I too have hung them up.

But not to your Sea Lord, I hang
my clothes to my Lady, Minerva.
She'll dry me off. Your love
was a watery grave.

Agnus

Lamb, I have seen you from trains.
I have seen you as I walked through fields.
You looked back at me, raised
your left hoof towards me in a delicate way.
Lamb, I have found your winter curls
by the roadside, on thorns and on barbed wire.

Lamb, who exalts what the world gets wrong
its failings, its struggles, honourable lamb
feel for us.

Lamb, all winter I wear black to absorb the sun.
Red is not as good at this. It is only for inside.
Lamb, my mother had a dream.
The whole family lived separately in sheds
in the back yard. It was dark and cold.
When we went to find each other, we weren't there.

Lamb, who exalts what the world gets wrong
heals wounds, smooths troubles, loving lamb
feel for us.

Lamb, these derelict testaments are stained.
They're cased in walls of clay. We cannot reach them.
We are damp and raucous, our marsh overgrown.
The trees under our pavements are dead. The stairs,
by which you left to sail up river, lead nowhere.
Lamb, why do we fear ourselves?

Lamb, who exalts what the world gets wrong
crowns hags, creates doubt, fragrant lamb
give us peace.

SARADHA SOOBRAYEN

Saradha Soobrayen received an Eric Gregory Award in 2004. She is a literature facilitator and the Poetry Editor of *Chroma: A LGBT Literary Journal*. Publications in which her poems have been published include *Wasafiri* and *Poetry Review* and the anthologies *This Little Stretch of Life* (Hearing Eye 2006), *I Am Twenty People!* (Enitharmon 2007), *New Writing 15* (Granta/the British Council 2007) and *New Poetries IV* (Carcanet 2007).

'Three moments' was first published in *This Little Stretch of Life*, 'My conqueror' in *Wasafiri* (vol. 50, Spring 2007) and subsequently in *I Am Twenty People!* and *New Poetries IV*, 'Sea patois' in *Wasafiri* (vol. 50, Spring 2007), 'I will unlove you' in *New Writing 15* and 'Marcus and me' in *New Poetries IV*.

I find the unquestioning nature of the dark comforting. Rewriting, rethinking and disbelieving usually take place in daylight. Most of the poems in this anthology were conceived in the dark. Writing at night, the poem's magic is assured, and uncertainties are welcomed. My concept of time changes at night; the writing also keeps its own time. Ten minutes goes by in a hour. The poems tend to explore different sensibilities by manipulating time 'Three moments' was an early poem that served as a springboard for later poems.

Written in the voice of an island, 'My conqueror' compresses 500 years of colonial history into one night of passion. In the poem 'Sea patois', voices are suspended between landmass and time zones – the past becomes present, the present becomes past. The images in the poem 'From the Closed Unit' misbehave within an unstable timeframe. 'Marcus and me' adopts a child's voice and a child's sense of time-specific imagery – 'catching the splashes, one drop, two drops' – while the handling of the future tense in 'I will unlove you' remains ambiguous – 'What becomes of us when love lets go?'

I aim to have a degree of ambiguity in the work and hope there is enough sincerity, clarity and particularity in the feelings conveyed in the poems to infect the reader. I like the idea of the 'infectiousness of art'. In *What is Art?*, Tolstoy discusses the distinction between 'counterfeit art' and 'true art', and describes how the reader becomes infected with the author's state of mind only when the work emerges from the inner need to express. What often resonates for me in the work is the need for something or someone, a sense of language not fully arrived at. The writing becomes a form of waiting.

Three moments

And today, playing with once was,
I have elasticised that glance,
stretched it past minutes,
and now a day or two passes
before we look away.

Later, I shall isolate
the area where your hand
swept my back. Scan
the friction under skin,
magnify the blood cells.

How brief, how soft, that
kiss. Tonight I shall freeze-frame
its contents: half a beat of
intention, a fraction of need
and a slither of desire.

I will unlove you

I will unlove you and become hollow,
undo every feeling from its hold.

I will restrict blood flow and circulate the cold,
deflate my heart and become shallow.

I will numb my tongue and choose not to swallow,
tie up my larynx, let love go untold.

I will scrub sensation from every fold.
and squeeze the tenderness from my marrow,

But will I still be your Saradha tomorrow?
What becomes of us when love lets go?

Marcus and me

Marcus and me like to wear
three jumpers to school.
The teacher tells me to say
the word 'warm' at least
seven times a day. But Marcus
says that warm is too small
a word, it moves away
too quickly like a mouse.

Marcus says that Anaemia
are little creatures, like lice.
He thinks he's caught them
by sucking the daisy foam
off my wallpaper.
Mum might have it too,
her pale face and kisses
taste of copper coins.

She doesn't mind Dad's
barking. Will it kill her?
Like her too-tight shoes or
an Asthma Attack? Marcus
sometimes hides outside
my parents' room. His ear
to the wall, his finger scraping
the paint off the radiator.

When Marcus and me have
an earache we go to my mum
and kneel like a donkey, my head
sideways on her lap, catching
the splashes one drop,
two drops. Mum rounds up
the wild hair from my ear but
her thumb can't shut out the thunder.

From the Closed Unit

Mum push me out,
wake me, take me home.
The cold space in my bed
is the ice cap of the world.
The seals are being stroked
then clubbed, their gulps
are torn, their wailing hardens.
I see women dragging their soon
to be born babies to hell.
They grab them back and throw
them in the air, up like dried
seeds, twisting out of sight.
A life is a life. Love quenches
these mothers, behind their eyelids
are pictures. After evening meal
why must you leave? Undo
these hospital corners.
The salt marks on my lips show
I am being nursed on marsh water.

My conqueror

She circles me with her Portuguese compass
and settles just long enough to quench her thirst.
She discards my Arabian name Dina Arobi,
and calls me Cerné, from island of the swans.

With the hunger of a thousand Dutch sailors
and a tongue as rough as a sea biscuit she stakes
a longer claim and makes herself comfy,
bringing her own Javanese deer, pigs and chickens.

Defending her lust for breasts and thighs, she blames
the ship's rats for sucking the dodo from its shell.
Looking past my ebony limbs, she sees carved boxes
and marron hands at work stripping my forests.

She renames me in honour of Prince Maurice
of Nassau. A good choice, sure to scare off pirates
keen to catch a bite of river shrimp, flamed in rum.
Disheartened by cyclones and rat bites, she departs.

For eleven years, I belong to no one. I sleep
to the purring of turtledoves. Sheltered by a circle
of coral reef, my oval shape rises
from the coast up to the peaks of mountains.

A westerly wind carries her back. She unbuttons
her blue naval jacket slowly and takes me.
I am her Île de France, her petit pain.
She brings spaniels. She captures marrons

who are pinned down and flogged, each time they run.
She takes her fill in Port Louis, shipping casks
of pure sweetness to the tea-drinking ladies of Europe.
Young Baudelaire jumps ship on his way to India.

His step-father wants to cure him of 'literature'.
Once a poet makes his mark, no tide can wash away
his words: 'Au pays parfumé que le soleil caresse.'
And what can I say, he was so delicious!

Sadly sweet Baudelaire soon finds himself
in such a profound melancholy,
after seeing a whipping in the main square,
after two weeks, he sails to France, leaving me

a sonnet. With the pride and jealousy of
the British Admiralty she punishes me
with her passion for corsets, sea-blockades
and endless petticoats wide as the Empire.

The oldest profession is alive and thrives
in my harbours; strumpets and exports, cross-
dressing captains and girls in white breeches.
Boys who like boys who like collars and chains.

She brings a pantomime cast of malabars
and lascars to my shores. Their passage back
to India guaranteed, if only they can read the scripts.
The cane breaks backs. Tamil, Urdu, Hindi, cling

to their skins like beads of sweat. Hundreds of tongues
parched like the mouths of sweethearts in an arranged
ceremony. She is kind and ruthless and insists
on the Queen's English. At night Creole verve slips in

and makes mischief. Each time she comes she pretends
it's the first time she has landed here, but she soon
becomes bored. Tired of flogging and kicking
the dogs. She doesn't know which uniform to wear.

'I'm no one and everyone,' she complains.
'And you have no more distinguishing marks
left to conquer.' She pulls down her Union
Jack; it falls like a sari, around her bare feet.

*Marrons: Creole name given to the slaves taken from Madagascar and transported
convicts. Malabars and Lascars: Hindu and Muslim indentured labourers. These
names are disparaging terms in Mauritian Creole.*

Sea patois

We had gestures, upside down feet, signals,
our bubbles crested into sea ash, our salt cooked
into yellow. We sheltered in a gasp,
a slip of dream. Our legs kicked out of sync,
interrupting the ocean's thoughts of fire-birds.

We were sunk, passed through amber and incense,
our lungs expanded starboard. We were burnt,
scattered backwards like unrefined sugar, our spirits
riding the deep pressure swells. Choked
on our own turquoise, we swallowed the horizon

and woke the half-eyed sun. Our love never
reached land, never discovered the New World
had weak ankles, tendons of dried seaweed.

FRANCES THOMPSON

Frances Thompson was born in Belfast and lives in Devon. Her work appears in magazines and anthologies in the UK, the USA and Ireland. She recently completed an MA in Poetry, with Distinction, at the University of Exeter.

'She' and 'Severance' appeared in *Reactions* 3 (University of East Anglia 2002). 'The Old Woman Wishes for a Road' and 'Severance' appeared in the Featured Irish Poets section of *Limestone: A Journal of Art and Literature* (University of Kentucky 2003). 'Matthew Godwin' appears on the Exeter Cathedral website: www.exeter-cathedral.org.uk/Poetry2.html.

'Severance' belongs with a series of poems about stone. It arose out of a conversation I had with a quarryman. I was struck by the feeling the man had for the material of his job. His descriptions evoked very different images of my own.

'Matthew Godwin' is one of ten poems I wrote in and about Exeter Cathedral. The Latin inscription that accompanies the carving of this fourteenth-century genius describes him as 'a pious and gentle youth'. All my cathedral poems came out in ballad form – the subjects, medieval for the most part seemed to require it. I also wanted to demystify their interesting, and often very moving, stories. Poems tend to shake themselves down into forms that suit the content.

Some years ago I was working on poems about water, and a woman emerged, 'her long hair flashing, her body white'. She stayed with me through several poems. 'She' is about her. She is fluid, and I am happy not to have trapped her; she belongs in that chaotic place at the back of the mind where poetry comes from. She is Heaney's 'fleeting glimpse of a potential order of things "beyond confusion", a glimpse that has to be its own reward'.

'Tantalaharna' and 'The Old Woman Wishes for a Road' both have, as a background image, a particular beach in Donegal. Tantalaharna has become a place of the mind, in which I am evaluating myself as a forger of poetry. I realised what the poem was 'about' after I had written it. The rhythm came first; the words entered the rhythm, and only when they were on the page did I see coherence in them. 'The Old Woman...' evolved in much the same way. Places can impose their own imperative.

Still with Ireland, 'Ur' harks back to love and loss against the background of the strictly divided community that was 1960s Belfast, before Larkin or even the Beatles had made an impression. The poem includes social and religious signifiers that anybody who was there will recognise, but they are not essential to the fairly timeworn plot. 'Airports' casts a colder eye on that same relationship from a more recent standpoint. I am trusting that such humour as can be read into it will outweigh its libel potential.

She

Like some forgotten foundling ghost
the white-bodied woman stoops and creeps
stirring my settled waters.

I am stalked in the dark by stories –
not of flawed Achillean heroes, or unicorns,
or people of dreams –

She is of herself, trailing ash and verdigris,
moving in poppy, heliotrope, verbena,
and wind-blown marigold.

She will not rest.
I will not invite her to rest,
to stir tea in a cup.

She knows the codling moth and the comma
and the milkweed, and the small dimpling hand
that my mother knows.

I turn from her – we have no common talk.
When I look, she has slipped
back to the water.

Severance

The man who is splitting stones
says that the rock,
in the moment before it breaks,
speaks –
gives a leathery *Yes*
along its agreed lines
of surrender.

I thought of how,
when you slice a carrot
lengthways,
it springs apart from itself
as if it has been waiting
all of its life
for this relief.

Sometimes, says the man,
you get smooth stone,
that does not so much crack
as slide apart
in great curved slabs.
I saw cooked codflesh,
gleaming.

He feels
he is granting a favour
to the damp virgin rock-face,
that has not yet
been frosted with dew,
or salted, or crusted
with lichen.

Matthew Godwin in Exeter Cathedral

In his ruff and scarlet gown
Matthew Godwin comes to town –
Master of the Music Scene
at the age of seventeen.

Though his gift was monumental,
Matthew pious was, and gentle,
with a genius unforeseen
in a lad of seventeen,

and the music he created
two cathedrals venerated.
Lord knows what he might have been
had he not died – at seventeen.

Now let Canterbury rejoice
that it once knew such a voice,
and Exeter hold the memory keen
of Matthew Godwin, seventeen.

Ur

After the first, there is no other.
It was like watching a good film in Czech,
or standing in an overheated gallery

before a Dali painting – the back of you
making for vanishing point, trees and leaves
whipping you along a pavement

that curled itself into a Boston sky.
The moment of it I didn't get for months.
Abraham probably stepped out of Ur

with the same sort of stride –
though with more company – not looking back
as you did not look back

not risking that last sight of a girl
in a newly Authorised Version of October wind,
her own personal translation,

and fending off already
her mother's 'What on earth's the matter dear?' –
the helpless hang of the Boys' Brigade tea-towel.

Airports

I used to think I saw you in Heathrow,
or in other airports linking with Belfast.
I thought sure that was you in Toronto,
and that time in Berlin. I saw you last

a hundred years or so ago, the cock
of your head and chin like this, your back set square,
the little hop and swagger of your walk,
Sweet Afton wafting in your breath and hair.

Oul greybeard fellas gazing into Guinness
in down-town cellars, is where you ought to be.
Can I believe this groomed insurance boss

grinning a website welcome? Pure Maths,
its probity, once provoked that grin. See
how the doors slide, the airport's empty glass.

Tantalaharna

I went to Tantalaharna
to be tried for the crime
of stealing words out of dreams
that were not mine.

As the Judge of Tantalaharna
passed me in his black silk
I touched the soft web of its weaving.
His face was oak

and mine a switch of willow
for words are not worth lives
though Tantalaharna was keening
in her stove-white waves,

and Tantalaharna was calling
You must keep the dreams that you stole –
yours are the words now
as my waves roll.

The Old Woman Wishes for a Road

Make me a road I can walk once more –
a road with white houses, on a white shore,

and there must be sand, banked well
and scattered, ground out of shell,

out of bone, out of stone in the sea's eye –
a road under rain, and a wind to dry.

Then I'll take to my road, and frailty flouting,
I'll hitch up my skirts, and I'll run, shouting –

I'll run with the children, shouting, shouting.

DAMIAN WALFORD DAVIES

Damian Walford Davies was born in 1971. He is Senior Lecturer in the English Department at the University of Wales, Aberystwyth. A co-authored collection of poems, *Whiteout*, was published by Parthian in 2006. A collection entitled *Suit of Lights* is forthcoming from Seren. The poems in 'Composite' were first published in *Poetry Wales* and *Planet: The Welsh Internationalist*.

There's a word for it – ekphrasis: the attempt to make a painting 'speak' in poetry. The enterprise has its dangers: the result can often be a mere exercise, a second-hand, even parasitic, engagement. And one's interpretive freedom is not a licence to thrill. The challenge is to make something that breathes its own creative oxygen, that communicates the original without merely replicating it, that expands its dimensons. For me, responding to a painting seems to kick-start processes that can have beneficial effects on the writing of other poems. Perhaps this is another way of saying that all poems may in some sense be responses to images.

I first saw John Knapp-Fisher's paintings in his gallery in Croesgoch, near St Davids, Pembrokeshire, about fifteen years ago. They excited me then, and continue to do so. That coastal region is beautiful and challenging in equal measure, and John's art, characterised by the seemingly antithetical qualities of starkness and mystery, resolutely resists the easily digestible touristic view. He's an experimenter in a range of forms, but his trademark images are of whitewashed farmsteads unnervingly, exotically luminous against a background so dark you feel its gravitational pull (hence 'tradematt/absence of the dark' in poem 2 and the image of deep space in poem 7). I chose ten paintings from John Knapp-Fisher's *Pembrokeshire* (Senecio Press 1995 and 2003) that seemed to encode a secret or suggest a narrative to be unlocked. The 'Composite' sequence is full of questions and words like 'perhaps', marking the attempt to feel around these images. Strange absence or excess of light, and figures ambiguously located in a landscape, render these paintings disturbing.

So foliage seems a 'threat' in poem 1; the figure in poem 2 exits into 'strange weather' like a scapegoat; the tree in poem 3 betrays the artist's worry; agricultural work becomes Sisyphean in poem 4; we're faced with a choice between life and death in poem 5 and with another primal choice in poem 6; the farm buildings in poem 7 are both Welsh vernacular and cosmic oddity/odyssey; the ghostly illumination of a coastal village by a late sun or winter moon in poem 8 becomes atomic 'after-/blast'; a fall is always possible for the figure crossing the bridge in poem 9; and the rape field of the last poem is filled with 'yellow violence' and mysterious signalling. And I wanted to give a sense of the strange pressures – of reality, of possibility – exerted from beyond the frame.

Composite

1 Gill in a Pembrokeshire Lane

The threat of foliage; the girl
caught in the painter's headlights, but
looking as if she's about to
draw.

2 Llanwnda (c. 1985)

I know – I mean
from afterwards being
there – that off right there's
a church you've painted
elsewhere. Here, only a fore-
shortened midnight
village against that tradematt
absence of the dark: white
rambling house; the hayloft
converted later
by your son. And then

that man, a suggestion
of a stoop, sent out
in your strange weather
like a scapegoat, looking right
outside the frame: because
somewhere there, perhaps in
light, you've placed the church.

3 Fisherman's Shed, Porthgain

See, from the trees, the
prevailing wind? The road
tacks right, under a sky
you've worried over, under a tree
that wind is bent on
corrugating into winter.

4 Tractor on a Skyline

March, perhaps. Cold
enough for the exhaust
smoke to hover over
the caged driver, who sees,
without vantage, the wide
expanse of all the work
not done.

5 Houses – Cardigan

Someone on each thresh-
old, like doors: watching

what? The carnival or
funeral is beyond the shaker
frame.

Difficult in all this noise and all
this silence to make
out whether

those squares are chimney-
stacks continuing the line, or purged
sheets strung
wet across the street.

6 The Birthday Walk

Eliot's insistent lane. Follow
them, then, along that patch-
work camber – whether down or
up is left up or
down to you.

7 Manor Farm

Amazing – that medley
of roofs hung
in feudal deep space.

What language will those
three, docked
in that capsule of a porch,
speak?
What will the martins,
returning to de Gower's
farm, breathe?

8 Abereiddi Evening

Sudden ill-
umination,

like a bomb going off, off
left, as in fifties news-
reels from Pacific tests where
soliders in shorts, like kids
at the end of their count, turn
to face the stunning after-
blast, and a very English
voice makes absolute
sense of it all.

Here, white-
blast cottages at dark,
and a street
lamp like a question-
mark, enquiring whether
anyone's left to watch.

9 Nevern Bridge with Figures

Frail, now, and drawn
delicately as the curve
of the bridge;
the hand that is not in his
extended to anticipate
a fall.
                    She should know
that where this image ends
the road begins
to climb, though her poise
suggests she'll cross that
bridge when she comes to it.

10 Girl in a Rape Field

Yellow violence: the scare-
crow girl fending
off the crop; tyre
tracks converging
to an accident.

Yellow violence; her patch-
work skirt a minor
landscape, her
semaphore bringing whom
in over the dark
cairns to land?

The paintings are from John Knapp-Fisher's Pembrokeshire *(Senecio Press 1995; 2nd edn 2003).*

JOHN WHITE

John White was born in County Londonderry. He completed a degree in English at Oxford University, and has worked variously as a civil servant, teacher, and since 1999 as a special educational needs officer with Oxfordshire County Council. He recently completed a Masters degree in Creative Writing, also at Oxford.

'Also Like Him' first appeared in *Oxford Magazine*.

When it comes to influence, familiar names (Elizabeth Bishop, Simon Armitage) and subjects (life, death) figure strongly. But I must also confess to a little local bias. Robert Frost once said: 'you can't be universal without being provincial…it's like trying to embrace the wind'. So I veer towards the 'local', a productive practice in recent Irish poetry, though not without its dangers. The novice poet can flounder, crudely aping the concreteness of Seamus Heaney, the linguistic play and pattern-making of Paul Muldoon. Early on, I found myself repeatedly writing about the place where I grew up in poems filled with local 'things' and 'rings' whose purposes were unclear to me. The 'obscurantist' Muldoon is instructive, promoting the 'primacy of unknowing' for the reader of poetry, while insisting on 'almost total knowingness on the part of poet as first reader'.

'Lyrical Ballad' was an early effort which, reading back, contains fragments rather than things. Based only slightly on a man I once knew but whose name I pinched, its proverbial bits come mainly from my mother's farmhouse upbringing and an oral culture sadly drifting away. The impetus for that poem was an obscure proverb, but there are many spurs. Painting is another, and 'Desire', based on a canvas of that name, is a sort of homage to Stanley Spencer, who elevated the primitive and the plain to saintly status. In the case of 'Work', I juxtaposed a postcard (an alpine scene) with a curious occupation (topiarist) to carve out something both surreal and familiar. The subject appears to me now as a sort of demented Calvinist figure (which, with my background, is very familiar).

Travel can also inspire, in unexpected ways. 'Mole' began as an attempt to recapture something of the city of Oaxaca. But a poem based on a Mexican sauce ends with potatoes: somehow the 'local' seeps into everything I do. 'Special' takes a famous line from Shakespeare and speculates on how it – and the world generally – might be interpreted by a child with a learning disability. That's partly based on my day job, but also on a cousin with Down's Syndrome. Finally, 'The Gentler Engine' and 'Also like him' are inspired by my father. Once I had decided on the form, these poems virtually wrote themselves, which doesn't happen often. Why I write I'm still not sure. But I take my inspiration wherever I find it, knowingly or otherwise.

Special

The quality of mercy is not strained:
I like that line, I copied it several times
until Miss said James what's that you're writing?
What have you been drawing? How marvellous,
the way you've got that cloud, which is
a cloud I take it – I know you love outside.

I said I didn't today, it was dangerous,
the trees were shaking out the birds like dandruff
and the sky was growing dark like Jason's face,
smudged like charcoal (he's begun to shave).
It was dangerous for Jason too. She smiled –
You chose the wrong behaviour. What she meant

was why did I hit him, or write the same words
line after line. Was I starting to get bored?
No, Miss, but I don't like being stared at
for one thing, and this cloud is a head of steam
in Mummy's kitchen. And this hat's a pot
and on the sideboard is a radio, it just seems

like it's a picture or a painting but you see
it is the singer's face, who one day will be me.
There's a girl at school like me who's got fat hands,
she wanders slowly round the boundary fence
and smiles sometimes, as if she's almost happy.
Most of the time I don't know what to say.

I didn't know you sang, James, that's a treat.
You have an ear for music, you're really very bright.
Is not strained, I said, are the words you can't make out
and the Quality of Mercy is the dish I've made.
As for this drop of sauce that looks like blood,
be careful Miss, it'll end up on your head.

Work

Into the Alpine valley
sailed the topiarist
with his book of prototypes,
leaving inky strokes
across the Piedmont snow,
beyond a lone bare tree
its branches groaning
on his upward journey.

Trying to stay warm
he pictured desert slopes
where honey oozed
and locusts crept along
the rim of the eye,
then getting high enough
to start into his labour
seized his instrument

and with a flurry of air
and snow began to carve
not saints or noble beasts
but, with compass in hand,
a clock tower, castle,
ark and a giant barn,
pruning the objects until
they shone like crystal

and it was only as he relaxed
that the blood appeared
in painterly flecks
on the alpine snow
beneath his spotless shears.
He pondered as he bled
that he would cut himself
he was so sharp they said.

Mole

After the capital the pace had slowed
(which we judged more the ticket)
though the trumpets in the Zocalo
proclaiming civil rights for Zapotec
and Miztec pummelled us with so much noise
you could have taken it for the Twelfth –
the drums, the stocky men with sweating brows
marching, stumbling in undulating rows.
Time for hungry tourists to catch breath,
to rationalise it all in film and prose.

My diary entry states the skies were bluer
here and though this snap corroborates
the polished pen, I look as if I'm blootered.
Bare-legged we're two separate races
thrown together accidentally
in far Oaxaca, and for all we've tried
to shuffle on another skin (here's me
with my Fuentes novel) I have to say
we didn't convince a sinner – we who'd shied
from ordering a dish containing Mole

which we find to be a sort of paste,
the colour and consistency a bit
like clabber (not, thank God, the smell), its taste –
depending on the menu – sweet
or spicy, sometimes both together,
with a role so various
a trowel load might soon repair
adobe walls, or whatever you suppose
in need of mending (round this shady square
right here) unlike, let's say, potatoes.

Desire

(*Stanley Spencer, 1933*)

So, there's a difference in height,
Some say she looks too big for me.
They all are wrong and I am right,
We're tokens of fidelity.

Some say she looks too big for me,
'*She squints at Stanley from above*'.
We're tokens of fidelity,
The apotheosis of true love.

'*She squints at Stanley from above*'.
Her dress is lumpy, old and seamed,
The apotheosis of true love.
Yes, ugliness can be redeemed.

Her dress is lumpy, old and seamed,
Still I gaze longingly at her.
Yes, ugliness can be redeemed,
Whatever clothes she deigns to wear.

Still I gaze longingly at her,
Her face is bathed in heaven's light.
Whatever clothes she deigns to wear
I clutch her arm, I hold it tight.

Her face is bathed in heaven's light.
So, there's a difference in height.
I clutch her arm, I hold it tight.
They all are wrong, and I am right.

The Gentler Engine

My mother says 'it was his stethoscope'
that told him finally it was time to stop.

At sixty-five, but ready to go on,
his hearing was the thing that let him down.

He'd catch the heartbeat of a countryman
alright, but not the murmur in a wean.

He'd greet at that, pop next door to consult
his colleague, check that what he'd seen and felt

could be attested. And he knew the buck
would rest with him. The gentler engine's tick

was fading fast, less audible each year
even those higher notes – a lorry changing gear,

the siren blast, the crack at close of play.
The sitting room grew quiet, as did he.

'Just like *wer* dad' is how she's painting it,
though with his genes I feel a touch splenetic.

I say 'Sometimes, already I sit mute
at parties, meetings. What hearing I've got

will pass the test, no doubt. The sort of stuff
I do is not exactly life or death.

Today's professionals smile a lot and listen
to gabble.' 'Aye John,' she says. 'Just like him.'

Lyrical Ballad

A hired horse,
the old man
Willy Loughridge said,
scraping lumps of ash
into the grey Bann,
is never tired.

He had only got
the two teeth sitting
in his head,
to which rough hands, cut
from years of pulling
flax, had pointed

but they were
he thanked the Lord
furnenst ayther,
the soft burr
of his every word
floating hither and thither

in the flapping wind.
Shivering you felt
he would prophesy
till it *wud have skinned
a fairy* or he smelt
it was time for tea.

Uprooted plants
and debris drifted
along the river's back
as Willy advanced
(it's time I shifted)
further up the track.

Also like him

The slow tramp to the kirk, the laying down
is done now. Folk drift down October lanes.
The Book says *man goeth to his long home* –
a dark-eyed house with heavy-lidded panes.
That spirit-quickening psalm of yesterday
ignited even my raw stuttering breath;
now clacking crows cloaked in a parody
of mourning fill the expanding emptiness.
This 'emptiness', the door shut to the street,
is habit-forming, soon solidifies,
or so I reckon, raking leaves, back straight
and (also like him) smiling with widening eyes.
Next door an engine revs up – labour of love.
A boy is playing 'Chopsticks' up above.

KIERON WINN

Kieron Winn was educated at Tonbridge School and Christ Church, Oxford, where he received a doctorate for a thesis on Herbert Read and T.S. Eliot. His poems have appeared in magazines including *Agenda, Oxford Magazine, Poetry Review, The Rialto*, and *The Spectator*, and in a short film about his work on BBC1. He lives in Oxford and is a freelance teacher.

'Wordsworth and Coleridge' appeared in *Poetry Review*, 'Unforgetting' in *The Spectator*, 'Ambleside to Glenridding' in *The Dark Horse*. 'The Gentleman Bowls Along' was first published as a hand-set leaflet from the Clutag Press, and read by the author on BBC1.

Author photograph reproduced by permission of Eleanor Sepanski.

'Wordsworth and Coleridge': the Wordsworths, at least in their time at Dove Cottage, would have porridge for two meals a day. Skiddaw is a particularly monumental mountain in the Lake District. One of the main causes of Coleridge's distress in their terrible falling out was the belief that Wordsworth had called him the last word in the poem.

'The Gentleman Bowls Along': I picture a man of the late eighteenth century who is marvelling at his 'pure organic pleasure' in seeing and moving. If we could all feel this all the time, there would be heaven on earth.

'Waters': this came from reading a 2006 interview with James Lovelock. It is not the planet that is (arguably) doomed.

'Unforgetting': my parents now live in Cornwall among the scenes of our family holidays. When I started to visit them there, long-forgotten knowledge returned to me. The process reminded me of Plato's theory of *anamnesis*, or 'unforgetting', in which spiritual knowledge is recovery of what the soul knew before it was incarnated.

'Mountain Water': the final rhyme would have been a full one for Wordsworth.

'Ambleside to Glenridding': this is a walk in the Lake District, from the town of Ambleside to a pub in the village of Glenridding, by Ullswater, the second-largest lake. A prospect, in eighteenth-century thinking, is a picturesque view. Rydal Water and Brothers Water are lakes, Fairfield is a mountain, and Scandale Beck and Goldrill Beck are streams.

Wordsworth and Coleridge

Insufficient, the broad
Oaten flakes,
The convictions plain
As Skiddaw –

How Coleridge would have loved
Neon, glutamates
And so many channels:
Intricate, hare-like, in the end a nuisance.

The Gentleman Bowls Along

for Peter Conrad

The gentleman bowls along, and flourishing his cane
Creates new symbols in the morning air.
His face is sanguine-pink, his waistcoat half unbuttoned;
His liquid eyes reflect stout cattle, orderly hedge;
His brimming heart spills some runaway laughter.
With happiness to hand in breathing, seeing,
Paradise for man cannot be far away.

Waters

Soon the environment may find these rooms
And seas come crashing through this private door;
Coral would be succeeded, strange bright plumes
Would come, and different kinds of mouth and claw,
Even if Nature's earliest conscious blooms
Were gone, and nothing left to weep in awe.

Unforgetting

Flat shining fields of sand, the shallow-carving
Tigris and Euphrates of the beach streams
Where individual flying grains are seen,
The wet compactions out of which grew keeps
I used to raze with greyish slapped moat water,
Enthralled and never doubting I was loved,
Blue-black rock, its surface softened by salt,
Like miniature coast the coming wave would ruin,
Caves that had ground no man had trodden – all
Stored when the soul passed here before this life,
Restarted by a sleepy train's long snaking.

Mountain Water

Lucid stream,
Travelling light,
Itself and open,
Black and white,
Cold on the palm,
Chilly burn,
By mossy rock
And thriving fern,
Salt and poison
Clouds remade,
Ancient freshness,
Undecayed,
Fluid muscle,
Inner chatter,
Flowing, constant
Mountain water.

Ambleside to Glenridding

for Amanda Holton

The eighteenth century notes Rydal Water
Glittering in a prospect. By Scandale Beck
Climb on a pony track past meteorite-grottoes
To High Sweden Bridge, a lone constructed eye,
A glimpse of civilisation, then press on
To a prehuman valley in the mountains
Networked by veins of thin and plashable streams.
Now up, an easy up, with Fairfield left,
Mist and moisture cool on grateful limb,
Loved wideness, thereness, love like sun on stone,
To a broken ridge, the start of dirty walking,
Oikish grass and ankle-killing holes,
But there is light and we have time and food;
So Brothers Water inches round a hill,
Lake like a flat grey pebble, and reaching earth
We head past waterfall and fiery fern,
Past Goldrill to the silver spill of Ullswater,
Its miles of absolute edge as mild as Jesus,
Then to the Travellers Rest for woods-floor beer,
Rich seasoned beef, potatoes piping, whisky
And shortbread, fire and sugar for the next day.

LYNNE WYCHERLEY

Lynne Wycherley graduated in English, Religion, Psychology and Art. She has worked in archaeology, wildlife conservation and second-hand books; she now works at Merton College. Widely featured in poetry journals, she was selected as an Alternative Generation Poet. Since her debut pamphlet (Acumen 1999), she has had two Shoestring collections: *At the Edge of Light* (2003) and *North Flight* (2006).

Of the poems chosen for this anthology, 'Caroline Herschel's Vigil' (runner up for the 2003 Frogmore Prize) was previously published in *Four Caves of the Heart* (Second Light 2004), 'Bewick Swans…' in *Earth Songs* (Green Books 2002), 'Tawny Owl' in *Poetry Wales* and the *Independent on Sunday*, 'Inhabiting a Distance' in *Poetry Nottingham*; the poems were reprinted in her collections.

Light; landscape; love. Light, its nuances and imagery, permeates my imagination and my words. Born on the edge of the Fens, I was influenced – perhaps unconsciously – by the contrast between black peat and the lit breadth of the horizon. It was a land steeped in waterfowl and saints, its rich fields accompanied by stark poverty. It flung open the doors of the sky, but it exacted a toll. John Clare had trodden the same soil. He was my reading companion, and still is.

All too rapidly, that early world became polluted and eroded. My creative journey is partly an eco-spiritual one: my first poems were published in the environmental journal *Resurgence*. Much that I celebrate both thins and intensifies against the rising threats to our biosphere. Mine is a kind of love poetry: for places, people, wildlife. At times, it is a rebellion against reductionism, a desire to articulate a larger response, whether to the pathos of a human face, or the unfathomable fire of a leaf, a gamete, a star.

In my twenties, I studied Western esoteric traditions. I cherished Emily Brontë, Kathleen Raine; but I was slow to begin writing. It was not until the mid-1990s, and the sudden death of my father, that grief catalysed me. An awareness of human fragility hovers behind my words. My poems often spring from a lyrical impulse. I try to listen as I write. I like to hear music, or cadence, in poetry, even if it is lightly stressed: I value this in the poets I love.

Recently, my poetry has been energised by the north. Orkney, Shetland: where broadband co-exists with Neolithic cairns, where Norse dialects weave with the wind. I find shorelines magnetic, the uneasy margins between known and unknown. My first full collection was called *At the Edge of Light*. I am still working at that edge.

Caroline Herschel's Vigil

i

Who but an angel can scale the stars?
The telescope aims its cannon.
I watch my brother climb the rungs.
He rains numbers, crumbs from heaven.
I scurry to collect them,
busy as a mouse at the ladder's base.

Each night he pans, rides meridians;
each day I sweat the figures
into sense and grind fresh mirrors,
speculum-metal worked from its cast,
the cambers smooth, exact.

I polish as if erasing myself.
Better this than the glass in the hall:
it cuts me at the neck. I see
a goblin, a pygmy shrew, the child
typhus wizened in its grasp.

ii

My thoughts sway on their lonely root,
buds on a thorn. The house
breathes round me, night's bloom.
I dream of a stranger with blue-white hair,
pristine, iconic, a flying star.

I tilt my face to the circled dark,
a porthole on the summer stars.
I search the archipelagos of space
for a flare among the rocks,
a tern's feather on black velvet.

The darkness swings its slow wheel.
I see a ghost – a blaze of frost
so blue it stops my breath.
Silking the sky for three brief nights.
Indelible. Touching my life.

Bewick Swans Arrive at Ouse Washes

Just when I think the winter has won,
a black book closing

on pages of light,
and the darkness sways on its haunches

like an impatient bear
scooping up silver minnows,

I sense an agitation in the sky,
long Vs trailing like pennons.

Altocirrus, the swans are as white
as the tundra they come from.

Their cries multiply. Their bodies
crash-land on the water

star after star after star.

Herring Girl

Lerwick 1920

Exported for summer, I was drunk
with sickness on the Pentland Firth.
The salt wood rose: women
in tarpaulin, sketched in rows.
A shore swayed its ginger-grey line.
In trios we were sent to our
one-roomed huts, a brown reek
oozing from the curers' yard.

6 a.m. at the pier. Shouts
from the steam-drifters. I wait
by the farlin's gulley, my hands
bandaged against the dancing knife.
Now it fills. Stacked scales. The twitch,
slither, of two thousand fish.
Arms red, sleeves rolled, we
slice the gills, spare the milt,

our knives working faster than needles.
Fifty a minute: the cut flesh falls.
Sma's, matties, fills. Layer
by filmed layer in a ravenous barrel.
We work in threes, parodies
of the goddess. Later I dream
the moon is a fish, her slit-throat
children staring from steel rivers.

We are the untouchables:
oil stains my skin. Fiddlers
raise a tune. I laugh with the cooper
but his eyes stray seaward.
At night my salt-douched sores
cry red. I slit flour-bags
to bind my fingers, tighten
the knots with my teeth.

Tawny Owl

The first time I met you, I was walking
on a hillside. You were a sculpture
in the cleft of a tree, waiting for
the sky to shut its yellow flower.

The leaves were a shaman's rattle
in the wind's dry mouth.
You peered at me from dreaming depths,
fawn barbules silking your body.

That night I thought of you
turning your head like a radar dish,
huge eyes in a Hallowe'en face
probing our shells, seeing

each loneliness, each twisting
gut of grief. I pictured the pulse
of your wings, softer and slower
than the systoles of our hearts

as you orbit like Pluto, patrolling
the edge of known and unknown
to alight on a blood-drop,
your talons spreading to a cross.

Each year I hear the bone flute
of your voice, hooked beak
blowing through a hole in stone,
calling the faint stars closer

calling *who? who? who?*
Your question hollows our mirrors.
The moon passes our windows
searching each face.

When I am old, I will step with
the Navajo through the cavern
of your voice. I will dress my bent body
in a shawl of chestnut feathers.

I will glimpse the night as never before:
cyan, hyaline, infrared.
I will swallow my brief life
and wrap its bones in velvet.

My thighs will thin to tarsars,
the horizon will shrink
to an astonished O
as my shoulder-blades open to the stars.

Inhabiting a Distance

There were days the sky lived in your eyes,
a late-winter light, white metal. Some said
you were remembering the war. Italy,
the desert. But I'd see the boy in you
and distance beckoning. Saturday fields:

how you'd flee from home, a camphor front room.
My grandmother calling, maddened, relieved
and dinner's at one! It won't keep.
Freed from a pipkin to a sea of peat,
Farcet Fen, Ramsey Mereside, the Nene.

After the war, those fields would restore
their bitter certainties. Potato-picking, ditching,
singling the beet. Your demob coat no proof
against the wind. A tractor clinging
to the skyline. Writing its one black poem.